T0294277

BEYOND
THE
PAPER

BEYOND
THE
PAPER

Selected Stories about CPPCC Proposals

Lai Ming

Books Beyond Boundaries

ROYAL COLLINS

Beyond the Paper: Selected Stories about CPPCC Proposals

By Lai Ming
Translated by Feng Lei, He Li, and Bai Wenkai
Revised by John Olbrich and Haiwang Yuan

First published in 2024 by Royal Collins Publishing Group Inc.
Groupe Publication Royal Collins Inc.
550-555 boul. René-Lévesque O Montréal (Québec) H2Z1B1 Canada

Copublished with Encyclopedia of China Publishing House

ISBN: 978-1-4878-1112-9

To find out more about our publications, please visit www.royalcollins.com.

Contents

Written on the Occasion of the Publication of the English Version of *Beyond the Paper: Selected Stories about CPPCC Proposals*

———————

What is a proposal? It is a kind of written opinion with suggestions submitted by the proposer to the plenary session or the standing committee of the Chinese People's Political Consultative Conference (CPPCC), examined and filed by the committee, and then sent to the relevant government departments for processing and response. This definition is made from the perspective of the work of the CPPCC. But if we look at it from the standpoint of a discipline, proposals can be regarded as a kind of discourse on politics, an official document that puts forward opinions and strategies. In ancient China, the imperial courts always took the discourse on polities as the primary focus when selecting officials through imperial examinations. Compared with literary elegance, unique and valuable insights define a good discourse on politics. In a discourse on politics, the author's analysis would target at a main issue such as current affairs, farming, folk custom, etc., and propose solutions to the issue in discussion. The essays "On the Mistakes of the Qin Dynasty" "On the Explanation of the Expensive Millet" "Suggestion of Ten Issues Worth Concern to Emperor Taizong" and "Strategies of the Warring States," written by ancient intellectual elites, are outstanding discourses that are concise but powerful and sophisticated. "On the Six States," written by Su Xun and Su Zhe in the Northern Song Dynasty, is another example. From the perspective of the concept of "potential" in Chinese traditional culture and military strategy, the essay analyzed how the six states relinquished their territories and power to the Qin State, in an effort to dissuade the then decision makers of the Northern Song Dynasty.

Therefore, different from the academic thesis, personal reflections, speeches, proses or work summaries, a proposal is a unique genre of discourse on politics. It is a problem-oriented and argument-centered article that proposes appropriate responses. This dissection of the definition of a proposal enables us to better understand the basics of a proposal (problems, analysis, and solutions). It is also a prerequisite for better understanding stories about proposals.

Stories about CPPCC Proposals

Proposals emerged with the establishment of the CPPCC. Over more than 70 years, proposals have played an essential role in the founding of the People's Republic of China (PRC) and the socialist revolution, construction and reform by adhering to the two primary themes of unity and democracy and serving the central work of the Communist Party of China (CPC) and the government. During the First CPPCC National Committee, a total of 193 proposals were received, which played a vital role in restoring and developing the national economy, realizing the general line for the transition period, enlivening the political life of the country, and adjusting the internal relations of the united front. During the socialist revolution and construction, CPPCC members put forward proposals on industry, agriculture, culture and education, science and technology, political and legal affairs, ethnic affairs, and the united front. When making decisions, the CPC and the government adopted many opinions and suggestions in those proposals. During the period of reform and opening up and socialist modernization, CPPCC members, CPPCC participating units, and special committees have put forward more than 110,000 proposals focusing on major economic and social issues and concerns of immediate interest to the people, which have played an essential role in promoting economic and social development. Since the 18th CPC National Congress, the work on proposals has focused on the overall layout of "the Five-sphere Integrated Plan to advance economic, political, cultural, social and ecological development" and the coordination of "the Four-pronged Comprehensive Strategy" (that is, to make comprehensive moves to complete a moderately prosperous society in all respects, to reform further, to advance the rule of law, and to strengthen Party self-governance). It is aimed at arriving at a consensus on major issues, which has made a notable contribution to the realization of the "Two Centenary Goals" (that is, to complete a moderately prosperous society in all respects by the centenary of the CPC founded in 1921 and to build China into a modern socialist country that is prosperous, strong, democratic, culturally advanced, and harmonious by the centenary of the PRC founded in 1949). According to statistics, by 2020, the CPPCC National Committee had received more than 150,000 proposals and handled 135,800.

In the face of a vast number of proposals and the intricacies of proposal work, the best way to clarify the historical context of the proposals and make them come alive and accessible from the archives is probably to adopt the common practice people use when conveying a wealth of complex information—telling stories. Stories do not prescribe principles, nor do they give conclusion or claim to tell the whole truth, but they are often honest. As a matter of fact, the tradition of telling stories began in ancient times. Thus it makes perfect sense to tell stories about proposals, for stories have their magic.

To constitute the proposal story, we have to dig from many facts. Among the vivid details of the proposals are stories of people from all walks of life, the twisted process of proposal making and handling, serendipitous and surprising discoveries, and seemingly impossible victories. Among all these details, what this book concerns the most is the proposers' opinions and how they conduct their analysis. The readers will learn about some deeds and thoughts of the proposers. Primarily this book is meant to reflect the thoughts of the proposers, for it is the thoughts that are the true essence of the proposal.

Karl Marx once said: "Of course the method of presentation must differ in form from that of inquiry. The latter has to appropriate the material in detail, to analyse its different development forms and trace out its inner connection. Only after this work, can the actual movement be adequately described." (Karl Marx, *Capital*, Preface). Marx here speaks of the dialectical relationship between the presentation and inquiry. Similarly, the storytelling of proposals is not a random presentation but is based on the compilation and study of thousands of proposals. First, the characteristics, rules, and methods of proposal work are summarized in the two books we compiled: *70 Years of Proposal Work of the People's Political Consultative Conference* and *Promoting Proposal Work of the People's Political Consultative Conference in the New Era*. Then, 100 influential and important proposals made since the founding of the CPPCC were selected under the guidance of relevant theories. On these bases, we started to compile these vivid stories to search for the logic of the proposal work. Therefore, the stories about proposals in this book will reflect the rules of the proposal work. Only by understanding, classifying, and practicing these rules can we identify, understand and write appropriate proposals.

Stories on CPPCC Proposals Are Heart Touching

The stories about proposals are heart-touching. Readers can empathize with the CPPCC members' sense of responsibility and love for the country through these stories. CPPCC members, as representatives of all walks of life, are primarily intellectuals, with the advantage of a pool of talent and intellectual density. In ancient China, the social classes were categorized as "scholars, farmers, craftsmen, and merchants." Although the analogy cannot be fully drawn, CPPCC members can be considered contemporary "scholars" in a sense. They always have a sense of mission and responsibility. They embody the intellectuals' learning, spirits, and underlying temperament, embracing the patriotic sentiment of "being the first to be concerned with state affairs and the last to enjoy oneself." They fulfill their responsibilities and promote moral governance and the country's development by undertaking investigation and research and submitting proposals.

As early as September 1949, when the First Plenary Session of the CPPCC National Committee was convened, the delegates put forward their opinions and suggestions on various construction work of the newly found PRC in the form of proposals. Among them, the proposals of "Requesting the United Nations General Assembly to Deny the Representatives of the Reactionary Government of the Kuomintang (KMT) by Urgent Telegram in the Name of the General Assembly" by Guo Moruo and other 59 members, "The Central People's Government to Study and Implement the Policy of Protecting Overseas Chinese" by the China Zhi Gong Party (CZGP), and "Requesting the Government to

Explicitly Set October 1 as the National Day of the People's Republic of China to Replace the Old National Day on October 10" by Xu Guangping on behalf of Ma Xulun, who was on leave due to illness, became the first proposal, the first party proposal, and the first motion in the history of the CPPCC respectively, having a significant political impact at home and abroad.

Let's review the work of proposals after the reform and opening up. The story of Hu Juewen, the then chairman of the Central Committee of China National Democratic Construction Association (CNDCA), and Hu Zi'ang, the then chairman of the All-China Federation of Industry and Commerce (ACFIC), was told in 1979, after a decade of devastation during the "Cultural Revolution" when China's economy was severely damaged, and labor employment channels were narrow. At that time, there were more than 20 million unemployed young people in China, including those educated youth who returned to cities from the countryside and those unemployed who stayed in cities. Hu Juewen and Hu Zi'ang, together with 80 CPPCC National Committee members, jointly proposed a proposal of creating and expanding employment at the Second Session of the 5th CPPCC National Committee. The proposal was highly valued by relevant departments. Appropriate policies and measures were introduced one after another. In 1979, more than nine million young people were employed. By 1982, the previously accumulated unemployed youth had been largely employed in most areas of China. Hu Juewen and Hu Zi'ang were also among the five old men invited by Deng Xiaoping to a hotpot dinner. The "Five Old Men" are Hu Juewen, the "Machinery Big Shot"; Hu Zi'ang, the "Steel Tycoon"; Rong Yiren, the "King of Textiles"; Gu Gengyu, the "King of Bristle," and Zhou Shutao, the "Tycoon of Cement" (Zhou was also the chairman of Tianjin Federation of Industry and Commerce). Deng Xiaoping listened carefully to the "Five Old Men" who put forward opinions to ensure the implementation of the policies for business people. Deng pointed out that it is crucial to effectively mobilize financial and human resources for China's modernization.

The stories behind the proposals are heart-touching and impressive because the spirit of seeking and pursuing truth from facts of the CPPCC members can be easily felt from these stories. Let's look at the story of Sun Yueqi and the Three Gorges Project. Controversies accompanied the Three Gorges Project since the day it was proposed, with many supporting and opposing voices. To answer the question of who contributed the most to the construction of Three Gorges Project, Pan Jiazheng, a famous water conservancy engineer replied, "Those who opposed the Three Gorges Project made the greatest contribution to it." Zhang Chaoran, the chief engineer of the Three Gorges also said, "These objections makes our construction more focused on scientific evidence and more perfect. Regarding key engineering projects, we will be enlightened if we listen to both sides. Thus, in the Three Gorges Project, we did take consideration of their advice in the construction process." By absorbing different opinions and overcoming the problems raised in the opposing views, the Three Gorges Project ensured its quality. Among them was that during the Third Session of the 6th CPPCC National Committee in March 1985, 167 members of the CPPCC made 17 proposals, individually or jointly, on the Three Gorges Project, suggesting that its construction should be carefully considered. In response, the CPPCC set up an investigation group for the Three Gorges Project, headed by Sun Yueqi, who organized a trip to the middle reaches of the Yangtze River for further research by experts from various fields. At the age of 92, Sun Yueqi led the team for 38 days, holding more than 40 seminars and writing a general report and six special reports on investment, flood control, navigation, power generation, etc. Later, the leading group of the Three Gorges Project held a series of meetings. As I remember clearly, at one of the meetings, I attended as a staff member of the Hunan Provincial Government, some representatives questioned, "Sun Yueqi once worked at the KMT Resource Committee. What good advice can he give?" Regardless, Sun Yueqi personally wrote a speech of more than 16,000 characters. At the end of his speech, the old man said in a grave tone, "As a 93-year-old member of the CPPCC, in line with the principle of 'long-term coexistence, mutual supervision, sincerity, and sharing weal and woe' and in response to the call of 'informed efforts' to strive to be a true friend of the CPC, I expressed myself frankly with a pure heart. If anything is wrong, I sincerely welcome criticism." The old man's innocent heart and the sentiment of "being the first to bear hardships and the last to enjoy comforts" deeply touched every participant.

These are a few cases I picked randomly from the pool of proposals. Whenever I read these stories, I am deeply moved by the various deeds or remarks of the

CPPCC members: they have noble characters, pure spirits, strong minds and humble manners. The practice of proposal work proves that the CPPCC, with members as the main body, is indeed at the frontiers of cohesion, decision-making, consultation, democracy, and national governance.

A Story on a Proposal Is Also a Story on CPPCC

As Proposal work is an integral part of the work of the CPPCC, telling the story of proposals is to tell the story of the CPPCC. As the saying goes, "A drop of water can reflect the light of the sun." We summarize the experience of proposal work and then explore the laws and methods of this work by telling stories of proposals. So, over the past 70 years, what can we learn from the work of the proposal? This is: we must adhere to the CPC's leadership throughout all aspects of proposals and ensure the correct political direction of the proposal work by effectively implementing requirements of proposals issued by the CPC and enhancing the "Four Consciousness" "Four-Sphere Confidence" "Two Maintenance"; we must adhere to the deep study and thorough application of the CPC's innovative theories, in order to effectively take the latest achievements of Marxism's sinicization as the fundamental guideline and action guidelines for the proposal work; we must adhere to the nature of the CPPCC, play the role of the CPPCC as an important channel of socialist consultative democracy and a particular consultative body, and effectively perform its functions of political consultation, democratic supervision and political participation; we must keep strengthening ideological and political leadership and widely reaching consensus in all aspects of proposal work, and effectively carry out the mutual coherence of promoting democracy and enhancing unity, and make efforts in both directions to propose political ideas and reach consensus; we must adhere to the basic policy of focusing on the central work and serving the overall situation, take the realization of the "Two Centenary Goals" as the direction of performing our duties, promote the solution of unbalanced and inadequate development as the focus of our work, and focus on the proposals on key issues and major problems; we must stay people-oriented, take the realization, maintenance and development of the fundamental interests of the people as the starting point and anchor point of our proposal work, focus on promoting the improvement of people's livelihood, and assist the CPC and the government in promoting the people's well-being; we must adhere to the consultation and democracy throughout the work of proposals, effectively take consultation as the basic method and a necessary skill in submitting, filing, delivering, handling, supervising and giving feedback to proposals, and strive to enhance understanding, research consensus and promote work in communication; we must keep improving the quality and efficiency of the proposal work; we must keep improving the institutional mechanism and the system which is based on the CPPCC Charter and regulations about proposal work; we must continue improving the abilities of CPPCC members to perform their duties and teach them to better understand the CPPCC, be good at consultation, observe discipline and moral standards, in order to improve their competence in political awareness, investigation and research, engaging with the people, and cooperation.

"The more you know, the more decisive your actions are; the more you do, the more confident you are." The experience mentioned above can guide not only the work of proposals but also the whole work of the CPPCC in a greater sense. So we must adhere to and develop it.

Telling the story of proposals is only one of our pursuits. We also have a higher pursuit, that is, to further tell the story of the CPPCC through telling the story of proposals. As socialism with Chinese characteristics enters a new era, the system of the CPPCC will enter into a new period of greater maturity and stabilization. How can we give full play to the role of the CPPCC as a special consultative body of socialist consultative democracy and an essential part of the national governance system? How can we make the effective operation of the CPPCC as an institutional arrangement with Chinese characteristics to highlight the characteristics and advantages of China's socialist democratic politics? How can the CPPCC system be more mature and definite and contribute Chinese wisdom and methods to scientific socialism and humanity? These are questions to answer when we tell the Chinese stories to domestic and international audiences. By telling the story of the proposals and the CPPCC, we can clarify where the CPPCC comes from, where it is and where it is going, and explain what the CPPCC should be and how to build it in the new era. Only in this way can we shoulder the political responsibility of practicing the arrangements and requirements of the CPPCC issued by the Central Committee of the CPC and of bringing together the wisdom and strength of all Chinese, at home and abroad, who are striving for the great rejuvenation of the Chinese nation. This is the political responsibility of the CPPCC.

It seems we have a long way to go in storytelling, and we must go on telling stories of proposals and those of the CPPCC.

(Prefaced by Liu Jiayi, deputy director of the Cultural History and Learning Committee of the CPPCC)

Abbreviations

ACFIC	All-China Federation of Industry and Commerce
ACWF	All-China Women's Federation
ASEAN	Association of Southeast Asian Nations
CAGS	Chinese Academy of Geological Sciences
CAPD	China Association for Promoting Democracy
China CDC	Chinese Center for Disease Control and Prevention
CCJS	Central Committee of the Jiusan Society
CCPIT	China Council for the Promotion of International Trade
CCPPR	China Council for the Promotion of Peaceful Reunification
CDL	China Democratic League
CFEC	Central Financial and Economics Commission
CNDCA	China National Democratic Construction Association
CNR	China National Radio
CPC	Communist Party of China
CPPCC	Chinese People's Political Consultative Conference
CPWDP	Chinese Peasants and Workers Democratic Party
CUFTRA	China United Front Theory Research Association
CYLC	Communist Youth League of China
CZGP	China Zhi Gong Party
GBA	Guangdong-Hong Kong-Macao Greater Bay Area, shorted as the Greater Bay Area
GPEI	Global Polio Eradication Initiative
GPRD	Greater Pearl River Delta
HHS	United States Department of Health and Human Services

ICU	Intensive Care Unit
ISO	International Organization for Standardization
MOF	Ministry of Finance
MOST	Ministry of Science and Technology
MSAR	Macao Special Administrative Region
NBS	National Bureau of Statistics
NCHA	National Cultural Heritage Administration
NDRC	National Development and Reform Commission
NPC	National People's Congress
PHEIC	Public Health Emergency of International Concern
PKUHSC	Peking University Health Science Center
PRC	People's Republic of China
PRD	Pearl River Delta
RCCK	Revolutionary Committee of the Chinese Kuomintang
RUC	Renmin University of China
TDSL	Taiwan Democratic Self-government League
UN	United Nations
UNESCO	United Nations Educational, Scientific and Cultural Organization
UNICEF	United Nations Children's Fund
US CDC	US Centers for Disease Control and Prevention
WHO	World Health Organization
WTO	World Trade Organization

BEYOND
THE
PAPER

1 The Proposal on Abolishing Agriculture Tax

PROFILE OF THE PROPOSERS

XU KUNYUAN, born in November 1941 in Changshu, Jiangsu Province, is a member of the CPC and a professor-level senior engineer. He became vice president, CPC deputy secretary, and secretary of the Discipline Inspection Commission of China Textile Industry Association in 2001. He was a member of the 10th CPPCC National Committee.

ZHENG ZUKANG (1947–2011), former vice president of Fudan University, was a famous statistician and management educator. He was a member of the 10th CPPCC National Committee, the Standing Committee of the 11th CPPCC National Committee, the Standing Committee of the Central Committee of Jiusan Society, and the director of the Counsellor's Office of Shanghai Municipal People's Government.

Responding to the Call of the Times, CPPCC Members Propose Abolition of Agricultural Tax

———

At the First Session of the 10th CPPCC National Committee in 2003, Xu Kunyuan and Zheng Zukang, two members of the CPPCC National Committee, upon thorough consideration and discussion, submitted their jointly signed "Proposal on Abolishing Agricultural Tax."

Background

The agricultural tax had been in place in China for thousands of years before its abolition. China used to be one of the only two countries in the world that still levied the agricultural tax, the other one being Vietnam, and the tax on each hectare of land was close to USD 200 in China.

On June 3, 1958, the 96th Session of the First Standing Committee of the National People's Congress (NPC) adopted the Regulation of the People's Republic of China on Agriculture Tax. From that date on, the agricultural tax, as an important tax of the country, became a tax levied on all institutions and individuals engaged in agricultural production and earning agricultural income. The agricultural tax has distinctive features—it has agricultural income as the object of taxation and average annual output as the tax base, and is collected in kind and/or in cash; the tax rates, under the unified control of the state, differs by region; and local governments have much power in terms of its management.

Based on these features, the agricultural tax, upon its inception, was collected in kind in many places, i.e., in the form of grains or other main products instead of money; and collection was largely carried out by rural officials. Therefore, people commonly called this tax "public grain."

"The agricultural tax played a crucial role in the process of China's economic development," explained an expert at the School of Finance, Renmin University of China (RUC). "The tax revenue was mainly used for the development of community-level power organs and rural affairs, which was greatly helpful as China relied much on agriculture and was quite weak financially at the time."

Undoubtedly, the agricultural tax won space for China's development in a special period, and millions upon millions of Chinese farmers made indelible contributions to the development of China.

With the passing of time, however, it was found after decades that the rural tax system in those years was created under an urban-rural dual structure, running in parallel with the urban tax system. Such a tax structure imposed on Chinese farmers an unfair tax burden. Why was it unfair? Wen Tiejun, a noted expert in rural affairs, once explained in an interview: "With such a tax structure, the tax is levied equally on farmers whether or not they have an income, and regardless of age—a 100-year-old senior, or a newborn baby, everyone has to pay the tax on equal terms."

Once the drawbacks of the agricultural tax came to be known, well over 40 years after it was put in place, calls for cutting and even abolishing it, emerged first mainly among farmers and then, by about 2000, from some local officials and economists. CPPCC members at various levels, especially Xu Kunyuan and Zheng Zukang, were among the proponents.

Just as Xu Kunyuan and Zheng Zukang stated in their proposal, thanks to economic and social development, farmers' living standards improved, and their burden decreased. From 2000, a pilot reform on rural taxes and fees was initiated. Later, the reform was extended to 20 provinces in 2002, leading to an average of 30% reduction in the burden of farmers. The country invested RMB 30.5 billion in the reform in 2003. In comparison with cities, however, rural development was slow and farmers' incomes remained low. In 2002, while urban households had a disposable income per capita of RMB 7,703, rural households had a per capita net income of RMB 2,476. From 1997 to 2002, urban per capita income grew by 8.6% annually on average, but the growth rate was only 3.8% for rural areas. To increase farmers' income and reduce their burden is vital for rural economic development, improvement of farmers' living standards, stability in rural areas, the effectiveness of our efforts to expand domestic demand, and China's economic and social development on the whole.

"To stop levying the agricultural tax is a simple but effective solution to reducing the burden of farmers," Liu Feng, a CPPCC National Committee member from Zhejiang, also suggested straightaway in an interview. He added that the agricultural tax took a very big share in the country's tax revenue in the past, whereas with industry and commerce being the dominant part of the national economy, taxation in the country should accordingly focus more on cities or other sectors rather than on agriculture.

The Proposal

People began to call for the abolition of the agricultural tax in around 2000, but there remained the question whether it was the right time to do so.

Xu Kunyuan and Zheng Zukang conducted a thorough investigation and analysis before putting forth their proposal, and concluded that given China's huge population and limited farmland—less than one *mu* (approximately 667 square kilometers) per capita—farming generally served only as social security for farmers, with very small agricultural surplus. For urban residents, in comparison, under the country's market-oriented economic conditions, the personal income tax had a threshold of RMB 800 in monthly income. Statistics showed that in 2001, about 730 million farmers earned an annual net income of no more than RMB 4,000 and only less than 60 million earned more than that; in other words, most of China's farmers earned an income that was below the threshold of personal income tax of the urban residents.

"Agriculture is a weak-value sector, and up to now nearly all developed countries still provide, to varying degrees, financial subsidies and other protection measures for agriculture. Agriculture is still quite backward in China, and its input is far from adequate. Abolishing the agricultural tax, in effect, amounts to increasing the country's input into agriculture and, at the same time, avoids conflicting with WTO rules on agricultural subsidization." Zheng Zukang explained at the time. Moreover, the fact was that the tax and fee burden on farmers then was about RMB 120 billion, including over RMB 40 billion in agricultural taxes; the problem of rural debt was more serious with the national average debts of RMB 4 million for townships and RMB 200,000 for villages. The agricultural tax was detrimental to farmers recuperating from toilsome labor and thus hampered rural economic development to a certain extent. As a matter of fact, it was somewhat difficult to collect the agricultural tax in some places and the relationship between farmers and local officials was undermined.

Some people feared at the time that abolishing the agricultural tax would do harm to the country's "pocket." In response, Prof. An Tifu, a doctoral supervisor at the China Financial Policy Research Center, Renmin University of China, made an estimate, holding that the time was ripe for the rural tax and fee reform, and it was affordable if the annual decrease in revenue was RMB 12 billion in the following five years. Even if agricultural tax exemption could cause heavy financial pressure on places relying on agricultural tax revenue for fiscal expenditure, the central government has the full capacity to address such a problem by means of transfer payments.

More importantly, Zheng Zukang believed, agricultural tax abolition would pave the way for large-scale land operations and accelerate the urbanization of agricultural population, and these, in turn, would revitalize land resources transfer and help narrow urban-rural gaps and boost domestic demand.

After weighing the advantages and disadvantages, Xu Kunyuan and Zheng Zukang submitted this jointly signed proposal to the two sessions (the annual NPC and CPPCC sessions) in 2003. The proposal included a thorough account of the importance, timing, and advantages of abolishing agricultural tax, and made specific suggestions on how to advance it. They suggested, if it was financially difficult to abolish it once and for all, it could be done first in western China followed by the central and eastern parts of the country.

Follow-up

Shortly afterwards, the Ministry of Finance (MOF) gave a detailed reply to the proposal, acknowledging the views in the proposal and elaborating on what the Ministry had done and planned to do to address the issue.

In early 2003, Hu Jintao, then General Secretary of the CPC Central Committee, remarked, "Without *xiaokang* (moderate prosperity) for farmers, there would be no *xiaokang* for the nation; without rural modernization, there would be no national modernization. Fiscal expenditure allocation should in favor of the agriculture, rural areas and farmers." The "No. 1 Central Document" of the year was also themed on rural economic and social development.

On the afternoon of March 5, 2004, inside a small store in Dingfuzhuang, Chaoyang District, Beijing, a burst of applause was let out by seven or eight migrant workers from Hunan, Hubei and Sichuan, who were watching TV, tears in their eyes. Premier Wen Jiabao was delivering a report on the work of the government, and he announced that "from this year, the agricultural tax rate will be reduced by more than 1 percentage point per year on average, and agricultural taxes will be rescinded in five years."

At the very moment, perhaps many were as cheerful as these migrant workers. Premier Wen said, "The agricultural tax burden on farmers will be reduced by 7 billion yuan this year. All taxes on special agricultural products will be repealed except for tobacco, thus reducing the financial burden on farmers by 4.8 billion yuan annually. The central government will appropriate 39.6 billion yuan this year from its budget for transfer payments to support the reform of rural taxes and administrative charges." This aroused a new round of applause in the conference hall. At this moment, countless people across the country were overjoyed at the news, and Xu Kunyuan and Zheng Zukang were certainly among them.

This was the first time that the central leadership made a specific commitment on a public occasion over the issue of the agricultural tax, which also marked the central government's response to public calls and its commitment to deliver on it.

A promise made should be kept. The Chinese farmers began counting down to a new era where they no longer needed to pay the "public grain."

In the meanwhile, many also noticed that Premier Wen, upon announcing the abolition of the agricultural tax in five years, spoke of the necessity of accelerating supportive reforms relating to county and township administrative institutions. Zhang Xuedan, then deputy director of Tax Policy Research Office at the Research Institute for Fiscal Science of the Ministry of Finance, who watched Premier Wen delivered the report on television, saw significant connections here.

Repealing the agricultural tax could truly benefit the farmers and reduce their burden. But, simultaneously, it posed more urgent requirements for institutional reforms at the county and township levels. According to Zhang Xuedan, Some counties and towns must change the phenomenon of bloated institutions, because after the total abolition of agricultural taxes, the central government is already facing pressure—it is difficult to support some "idle institutions" and "idle people" through transfer payments. Moreover, since it was common for some local authorities to collect additional fees on top of the agricultural tax, it would be impossible to continue collecting such extra fees when the agricultural tax was abolished, and reform would be necessary at the basic level to regulate functions and performances of the authorities.

It is fair to say that the agricultural tax was abolished at the best timing, ushering in a new round of economic structural adjustments and reforms in rural areas, and injecting new energy for the country's economic and social development.

"State Tax Paid in Grains" Finally Abolished

The curtain was pulled open when in early 2004 Beijing announced the exemption of the agricultural tax and all additional charges, achieving "zero tax" in agricultural production processes. By estimates, this policy could benefit over three million farmers in suburban Beijing by more than RMB 80 million yearly. And previously Shanghai, Zhejiang, Jiangsu and some other provinces had already repealed the agricultural tax that had been levied for well over 40 years. One year after Premier Wen Jiabao promised in earnest in his government work report, on March 5, 2004, to rescind the agricultural tax in five years, 25 provinces, autonomous regions, and municipalities already abolished the tax, directly benefiting 730 million farmers by a few dozen or several hundred yuan.

Surprisingly, in 2005, far ahead of the five-year schedule he had promised, Premier Wen Jiabao announced at the Third Session of the 10th National People's Congress that the "state tax paid in grain," which had been levied in China for more than two thousand years, would be entirely abolished the next year. He said, "The agricultural tax will no longer be levied next year across the country. The originally planned goal of repealing the agricultural tax in five years will be achieved in three years."

This scene also left a deep impression on another CPPCC National Committee member, Wang Xiang, because during the CPPCC session of 2004—one year after Xu Kunyuan and Zheng Zukang submitted their proposal, he submitted a similar proposal and made his suggestions directly to the General Secretary.

It was 3:00 p.m. at China Resources Hotel, Wang Xiang recalled, that General Secretary Hu Jintao came to attend a joint group meeting of the China National Democratic Construction Association (CNDCA) and the All-China Federation of Industry and Commerce (ACFIC). At this meeting, Wang Xiang said, "General Secretary Hu, state tax paid in grain has been in place in China, an agrarian society, for over two thousand years. If it can be repealed unconditionally, it will be a great thing that benefits all generations to come." Wang Xiang suggested that while repealing the agricultural tax, the wine monopoly tax should be levied, which according to his rough estimation, can bring in over RMB 70 billion a year, far more than revenues from the agricultural tax, and this revenue could be used to make up for what local finance lost.

On that day, Wang Xiang told the journalist, General Secretary Hu Jintao mentioned him by name when giving a meeting recap, saying that the central government had been considering the issue. At the NPC conference the next day, Premier Wen Jiabao delivered his government work report and, when speaking of the agricultural tax, put down his report pages and stressed that agricultural tax rates were to be lowered step by step and the agricultural tax repealed within five years from 2004.

"In 2005 the Premier announced that the period for abolishing the agriculture tax would be reduced from five years to three years, and in his 2006 government work report, he made clear the central government's decision to totally abolish the agricultural tax in that very year. I was strongly stirred, and felt very proud," said Wang Xiang. Taking up the government work report of that year, he read, "This year we will completely rescind the agricultural tax throughout the country, a tax that China has been collecting for 2,600 years. This is a change of epoch-making significance."

"I've served as a CPPCC member for 14 years, during which time, I submitted about a hundred proposals. The agricultural tax proposal is what I'm most proud of," Wang Xiang told a journalist in an interview on the scene of the two sessions in 2006.

CPPCC members Xu Kunyuan and Zheng Zukang first proposed the abolition of the agricultural tax, CPPCC members Liu Feng and Wang Xiang made similar proposals later, and many other CPPCC members at various levels had consistently supported and called for burden reduction for farmers. Together, they were a driving force behind the abolition of the agricultural tax, and contributed greatly to this process.

In 2019, which marked the 70th anniversary of the founding of the People's Republic of China, the CPPCC National Committee commended 100 influential proposals made over the past seven decades. "The Proposal on Abolishing Agricultural Tax" made by Xu Kunyuan and Zheng Zukang was on the list. "The proposal embodies their sense of responsibility and enthusiasm for performing their duty of political participation, and their consideration about the national economy and the livelihood of the people," remarked Li Zhiyong, director of the Committee on Proposals of the 13th CPPCC National Committee.

This is an honor and a cherished piece of memory that belongs to the numerous CPPCC members, including Xu Kunyuan and Zheng Zukang, who contributed to the final repeal of the agricultural tax.

(Contributed by the Agriculture and Rural Affairs Committee, the CPPCC National Committee)

The Proposal for Eight Measures to Implement Reemployment in the Country

2

PROFILE OF THE PRINCIPAL PROPOSER

Hu Zhaozhou, from Wuhan, Hubei Province, was a member of the 8th CPPCC National Committee, vice chairman and CPC deputy secretary of the 8th and 9th Wuhan CPPCC, and former director of the United Front Work Department of CPC Wuhan Municipal Committee. He started work in September 1956 and joined the Communist Party of China (CPC) in March 1959. He has successively served as a member of China United Front Theory Research Association (CUFTRA), vice president of Hubei United Front Theory Research Association, vice president of Hubei CPPCC Theory Research Association, president of Wuhan United Front Theory Research Association, professor of Hubei Institute of Socialism and researcher of Hubei Specialized Committee for theoretical research of political parties. He has published monographs *On the Chinese People's Political Consultative Conference* and *On the Transformative Power of the United Front.*

Employment Is Pivotal to People's Wellbeing

───────

I n March 1996, spring was bright and vibrant. Deputies of the National People's Congress (NPC) and members of the CPPCC National Committee gathered in Beijing for the two sessions (the annual NPC and CPPCC sessions) in the year.

Professor Xiao Guojin, with a cheerful face and a few pages in his hand, came to me and said, "Director Zhaozhou, I have written a proposal. May I ask you for your opinions?"

Xiao Guojin, born in 1928, professor of Wuhan University and an economist, was a member of the 8th CPPCC National Committee, full-time deputy secretary general of Hubei CPPCC, member of the Standing Committee of Wuhan CPPCC, member of the Central Committee of China National Democratic Construction Association (CNDCA), vice chairman of CNDCA in Hubei Province and chairman of CNDCA in Wuhan.

At that time, I was a member of the 8th CPPCC National Committee, vice chairman and CPC deputy secretary of Wuhan CPPCC, and director of the United Front Work Department of Wuhan Municipal committee.

I worked with Li Chonghuai, Xiao Guojin and Gu Shengzu, the three chairmen of the Wuhan Municipal Committee of CNDCA for many years. I respect them very much. They have made important contributions to the reform, opening up and socialist construction.

After reading the original proposal written by Professor Xiao, I felt so appreciative and delighted. In my opinion, Professor Xiao's proposal with the eight measures of the reemployment project was in line with the spirit of the

Fifth Plenary Session of the 14th CPC Central Committee just held in September 1995 and it suited the actual situation of Wuhan's economic system reform. The value of this proposal lies in its combination of theories and policies and its embrace of predictability and feasibility. In my opinion, a political proposal must be feasible.

I asked Professor Xiao how this text was written in just a few months.

Professor Xiao told me that it was not a matter of a few months, but years of experience!

At the First Session of the 8th CPPCC National Committee held in March 1993, Xiao Guojin and several other members of the CPPCC National Committee put forward the proposal of "The Circle Center Theory—Building Wuhan into an International Market." "The Circle Center Theory" refers to the strategic idea of drawing on the advantages of circle radius in the market. Once the circle's center is prosperous, it radiates a long distance out into the neighboring areas, and the boom of the neighboring areas may then stimulate the central part again.

On April 18, 1993, Sun Qimeng (middle, vice chairman of the NPC Standing Committee and chairman of the Central Committee of CNDCA) made a special trip to Wuhan University to visit old friends of CNDCA, Xiao Guojin (left) and Liu Jingwang (right, famous calligrapher)

This two-way interaction continues. This development may turn Wuhan into an international market as it is connected with the growth of its vast hinterland in the surrounding suburbs and the Yangtze River Basin.

At the Third Session of the 8th CPPCC National Committee held in 1995, Xiao Guojin submitted a proposal for state-owned enterprises. His proposal focused on implementing the reconstruction project of state-owned enterprises running under deficit and starting renovation with the theory of "decay, fission and fusion." Its goal is to achieve a modern enterprise system, by giving full play to the principle of keeping public ownership in a dominant position and developing diversified economic sectors side by side.

This manuscript was the fruit of his years' hard work, which started from his proposal on "invigorating large and medium-sized state-owned enterprises" in 1988, continued all the way to the one on "the solution for state-owned enterprises running under deficit" in 1995. In order to write these proposals, he collected related materials with his own money. Though having no research fund, he willingly engaged himself in scientific study, participated in the deliberation and administration of state affairs, and managed to finish these proposals.

Professor Xiao's efforts moved me deeply. I understand that in order to establish the socialist market economic system, the CPC has gone through decades of exploration and struggle. And in order to find a solution for the reform of state-owned enterprises, thousands of workers from large and medium-sized enterprises have suffered, silently enduring great pain and making contributions to the enterprises reform in the country.

In that year, in accordance with the unified arrangement of Wuhan Municipal Committee, I made an investigation into the Wuhan Heavy Machine Tool Factory and the Wuhan Huanghelou Distillery with officials of Wuhan Municipal Committee and municipal government. I also led a team to Wuhan Building Materials Corporation and conducted research on the building materials industry for three months. I am well aware of the extreme importance of employment and reemployment projects.

I asked Professor Xiao if he had any other ideas. The professor said sincerely: "I want to make a joint proposal to ask Director Zhaozhou as the principal proposer. The joint proposal might be more likely to take effect with the signatures of Xu Qizhen and Tong Junmei." The professor also said that Jin Bintong, the full-time vice chairman of the Provincial Committee of CNDCA was very enthusiastic about the proposal and willing to sign it to show his support.

I expected Professor Xiao's intention of joint proposal when he shared me with his proposal. So I replied delighted: "I am willing to take the lead in doing this, but I have to make it clear from the beginning that this proposal was written by you, Professor Xiao—it represents your scientific research achievements over many years, and it is your intellectual property."

Professor Xiao and I talked and laughed, and the individual proposal was turned into a joint proposal.

Several members of the CPPCC National Committee in Wuhan were in different sections of the CPPCC and were staying in different hotels during the session. I immediately contacted them by phone one by one and reported the main points of Professor Xiao's proposal, and informed them that Professor Xiao was sincerely inviting them to make a joint proposal. They were very happy and supported the idea. They thought that this was a political event to care about the worries of the CPC and the State, and it was a good thing that would win the hearts of the people.

I joked with them on the phone and said that I would sign their names for them to save them a journey to my hotel. All of them happily agreed and thanked me. The joint proposal was completed in this way. I signed five names and the professor signed two names. This is why seven members seemed to have only two styles of handwriting on the front page of the proposal. The seven people involved were Hu Zhaozhou, Xiao Guojin, Jin Bintong, Xu Qizhen, Tong Junmei, Dong Guangqing, and Hu Heyan.

Those proposers were leading figures in their respective fields. Xu Qizhen and Tong Junmei were senior engineers in large and medium-sized key state-owned enterprises. They understood perfectly the background of the situation and agreed with the suggestions of Professor Xiao's proposal. In addition, both of them were excellent CPPCC proposers.

Until now, unfortunately several members including Xu and Tong have passed away. After 23 years, the joint proposal stood out from 140,000 proposals and won the honor of being among the 100 most influential and important proposals in the 70 years since the founding of the CPPCC National Committee.

Such an honor is great enough to comfort their spirit in heaven.

Professor Xiao submitted the joint proposal to the Secretariat of the General Assembly of the CPPCC, and I asked him to keep a copy of it for further reference.

I found that the proposal had a broad view on economic development. Professor Xiao believed that structural unemployment and technological unemployment would inevitably occur in the transformation of economic system from a traditional planned economy to socialist market economy and in the transformation of economic growth mode from extensive to intensive. This is a common problem encountered in world development. "The employment issue is a problem of economic development, an integral part of economic development, and it will be logically solved with economic development."

The proposal suggests that the government should take economic prosperity and full employment as its own responsibility, make employment the priority goal of national economic policy, and find a coherent approach to economic development and full employment, so that the vast majority of people could enjoy the fruits of economic prosperity.

After reading the proposal, what surprised me most was the professor's concept of mass employment and thinking about the way out of employment coherently.

He put forward the "double helix" employment approach for the first time. "The tertiary industry develops on the basis of the first and second industries. As the tertiary industry develops to a certain point, it integrates with the first and secondary industries, implements urban-rural integration, motivates emerging industries, and reaches a new level every few years to promote economic development and create productive employment opportunities." A cornucopia of employment opportunities will be provided with the integration of the first, second and tertiary industries in cities and in rural areas.

Late at night, thinking about my contacts with Professor Xiao over the years, I summarized three phrases about how to be a good member of the CPPCC, how to improve the quality of the CPPCC proposals, and how to use the CPPCC proposals to play the role of the CPPCC: careful topic selection, careful research and careful writing. This is the professor's character.

After submitting the proposal, Professor Xiao received the attention and support from the CPPCC Proposal Committee and its officers.

In June 1996, I received a very formal and sincere reply from the Ministry of Labor:

> *"Hu Zhaozhou and the other six members, we have received your proposal of 'Eight Measures for the Implementation of Reemployment Project.' Your proposal has thoroughly analyzed the practical situation. The measures put forward are of great value, have great inspiration and are very helpful for our work. The proposal also reminds us of responsibility for doing a good job in the area of employment."*

This was the first paragraph of the text, followed by a very serious briefing on the national labor and employment situation and the policies and measures to further strengthen the issue of employment. It was not just a simple reply, going through some figures and concepts. It constituted serious work on a critical issue.

Frankly, I was very moved by the reply from the Ministry of Labor. There are thousands of proposals at a session. For just one proposal, it is rare to draw so much attention. To this end, I replied officially: "We are very satisfied and grateful for the reply, and hope that national employment will have a new prominence and thus create new achievements."

On March 4, 1997, at the auditorium of the CPPCC National Committee, the CPPCC National Committee awarded certificates to outstanding proposals made by members from outside Beijing, which was an important part of the Fifth Session of the 8th CPPCC National Committee. Li Ruihuan attended and delivered a speech.

The CPPCC Proposal Committee asked me to make a speech at the meeting. In the early morning of March 5, I sent a press release to the Publicity Department of the Municipal Committee, *Changjiang Daily* and Wuhan TV Station.

This is the second time in history of the CPPCC that outstanding proposals were awarded honorable certificates. Since then, a five-year commendation system was instituted.

Among the 125 outstanding proposals were commended this time, five proposals were from Wuhan: the proposal "On the Strict Control of Bankruptcy

Case of Basic Industry Enterprise" by three members including Xu Qizhen; the proposal "On Rectifying Public Security around Wuhan Iron and Steel (Group) Company (WISCO) as Soon as Possible" by eight members including Tong Junmei, Wang Guangmei, and Hu Zhaozhou; the proposal "On Giving Full Play to the Advantage of the Direct River-Sea Transportation to Promote the Development of Iron and Steel Enterprises in the Middle and Lower Reaches of the Yangtze River" by Tong Junmei, Zhang Yongtai, Hu Zhaozhou Wang Guangmei; the proposal "On Strengthening the Management of Urban Migration Population" by Gu Shengzu; and the proposal "On Eight Measures for the Implementation of the Reemployment Project" by Hu Zhaozhou, Xiao Guojin, Jin Bintong, Xu Qizhen, Dong Guangqing, Tong Junmei, and Hu Heyan.

I wrote a few words on the honorary certificate issued by the CPPCC National Committee:

This is a masterpiece by Professor Xiao Guojin. Proposers: Hu Zhaozhou, Xiao Guojin, Jin Bintong, Xu Qizhen, Dong Guangqing, Tong Junmei, Hu Heyan.

Written by: Xiao Guojin
Beijing, March 4, 1997

After writing, I made a photocopy for each of them to keep as a memento of this glorious event.

On November 7, 2019, the 13th CPPCC National Committee decided to commend the influential and important proposals of the CPPCC National Committee in the 70 years since its establishment, and "The Proposal on Eight Measures for the Implementation of the Reemployment Project" was selected. This is a great honor for us. The fading past is like a puff of smoke. It has been 23 years since it was submitted.

Occasionally, I saw a short item of news in *Guangming Daily*, praising the influential and important proposals for the national economy and people's livelihoods, with the proposals listed, which impressed me deeply.

I read the proposal written by Professor Xiao and checked the documents of the National Congress of the CPC once again. It was like revisiting old times!

I found that from the report of the 16th National Congress of the CPC (2002) to the report of the 19th National Congress of the CPC (2017), there are chapters on the employment problem, which are deeply emotional, incisive and refreshing. You can feel the potential impact of Professor Xiao's theoretical research and policy suggestions on later national policies.

General Secretary Xi Jinping pointed out in the report to the 19th National Congress of the Communist Party of China: Employment is pivotal to people's wellbeing. We must give high priority to employment and pursue a proactive employment policy, striving to achieve fuller employment and create better quality jobs.

The policy on the priority of employment should be fully implemented. Employment is the foundation of people's livelihoods and the source of wealth. In 2017, the employment priority policy was placed at the macro policy level for the first time, aiming to strengthen the guidance of all parties to attach importance to and support employment. At present and for some time to come, the pressure on China's total potential employment level will remain unabated, structural contradictions are prominent, and new influencing factors are still increasing. Employment must be given more prominent importance. The primary role of steady growth is to ensure full employment. This year's new urban employment should strive to reach the actual scale of recent years on the basis of achieving the expected goals, so as to ensure full employment of urban labor force and leave room for the transfer to cities of surplus agricultural labor force. As long as employment is stable and income increases, we will have more confidence in the future of the country.

Food is the most important thing for the people. Labor is the source of wealth, and employment is the foundation of people's livelihoods. Employment is pivotal to people's wellbeing and the objective law of human social development.

On November 28, 2019, Hu Shuguang, member of the CPPCC National Committee, chairman of the Wuhan Municipal Committee of the CPPCC and secretary of the Wuhan Committee of the CPC at the symposium celebrating the 70th anniversary of the founding of the Wuhan Municipal Committee of the CPPCC, was pleased to announce that Wuhan had three proposals were commended by the CPPCC National Committee as influential and important proposals.

Chairman Shuguang awarded me the golden medal. I made a speech at the meeting. I said, "This is a collective honor for the Wuhan CPPCC, which has always attached importance to the work of proposals."

I have studied, and worked in Wuhan CPPCC and the United Front Work Department of Wuhan Municipal Party Committee for 31 years, personally experienced the proposal system of the plenary session of Wuhan CPPCC. Since 1996, I have witnessed how its procedures have been institutionalized and standardized. Successive secretaries of the Municipal Committee, mayors and chairmen of the municipal CPPCC have attached great importance to it, enthusiastically supported it, carefully organized it, taken charge of it, demonstrated the organizational advantages of the CPPCC, maintained its organizational role and improved it for 23 years—Wuhan CPPCC has created a miracle.

(Contributed by Hu Zhaozhou, member of the 8th CPPCC National Committee)

The Proposal for Promoting Reform of the Individual Income Tax System

3

PROFILE OF THE PRINCIPAL PROPOSER

The China National Democratic Construction Association (CNDCA), mainly comprises members from the economic circles.

The successive leaders and chairs of the CNDCA were Huang Yanpei, Hu Juewen, Sun Qimeng, Cheng Siwei, and Chen Changzhi. The current chairman is Hao Mingjin.

As of June 2017, the CNDCA has established organizations in 30 provinces, autonomous regions and municipalities, with a total of more than 178,000 members.

Promote the Reform of the Individual Income Tax System to Adjust the Distribution of Social Income Rationally

---

Personal income tax is levied by the State on the income of its citizens, individuals living in China and the income of foreign individuals in the country. It is one of the important forms of social redistribution. A rational and reasonable personal income tax system embodies social fairness and justice. In 2005, the Central Committee of the CNDCA submitted a proposal on promoting the reform of the individual income tax system to the Third Session of the 10th National Committee of the CPPCC. Since then, China's individual income tax system has been continuously adjusted and improved with the development of the economy and society, making important contributions to the rational adjustment of social income distribution and the promotion of harmonious and healthy development of society.

Development of the Individual Income Tax System Before 2005

In 1980, the Third Session of the 5th NPC passed the Individual Income Tax Law of the People's Republic of China and its implementation rules. This was the first tax law promulgated and implemented after the founding of the PRC, marking the official establishment of China's individual income tax system. At that time, the individual income tax threshold was set at RMB 800, and at the early stage of reform and opening up, the vast majority of residents' salary and income levels were far below this level, and the main tax targets were foreign enterprises and foreign employees in China.

In January 1986, the State Council promulgated the Interim Regulations of the People's Republic of China on Individual Income Tax for Urban and Rural Individual Industrial and Commercial Households; in September 1986, the State Council promulgated the Interim Regulations of the People's Republic of China on Individual Income Adjustment Regulations on the Collection of Personal Income Adjustment Tax for Private Enterprise Investors; in June 1988, the State Council promulgated the Provision on the Collection of Personal Income Adjustment Tax for Investors in Private Enterprises; in October 1993, the NPC passed the amendment to the Individual Income Tax Law, which carried out a comprehensive and systematic reform of the Individual Income Tax Law that had been passed in 1980, combining "one law," "two regulations" and "one provision" to form a more complete and unified individual income tax system. In January 1994, the State Council issued the Regulations on the Implementation of the Individual Income Tax Law, which stipulated that the individual income tax threshold should uniformly be 800 yuan. Income tax on wages and salaries was subject to nine levels of excess progressive tax rates ranging from 5% to 45%. Income from production and operation of individual industrial and commercial operations, and income from contracted and leased operations to enterprises and institutions were subject to five levels of excess progressive tax rates ranging from 5% to 35%. The other eight categories were all subject to a proportional tax rate of 20%; in August 1999, the 11th meeting of the Standing Committee of the 9th NPC amended the Individual Income Tax Law, deleting the item exempting savings deposit interest from individual income tax.

The Common Appeal of the Society to Reform the Individual Income Tax System

According to a sample survey on the basic living conditions of 290,000 urban households by the National Bureau of Statistics (NBS) in 2004, the per capita disposable income of urban residents in China in 2003 reached 8,472 yuan, an increase of 44.7% over 1999, while the low-income households whose per capita disposable income was less than 3,000 yuan accounting for 16.4%. In descending order of income level, the income ratio of the highest-income households to the lowest-income households of urban residents was 8.41, compared with 4.61 in 1999, and the gap had nearly doubled in five years. At that time, the Gini coefficient of the national income of urban and rural residents was 0.448, which exceeded the internationally recognized "warning line." It can be seen the gap between rich and poor urban residents in China is further expanding along with the rapid economic development. The function of individual income tax in regulating social income distribution has not been well played, and its role in narrowing the gap between the rich and the poor is weakening and lagging behind economic and social development.

The Central Committee of the CNDCA investigated this issue and found some problems in the individual income tax system at that time: First, it did not meet the requirements of economic and social development. The threshold for individual income tax on wages and salaries was RMB 800 per month, determined more than 20 years ago when the market economy was not significantly developed. After years of development, great changes had taken place in individual incomes, the market economy, prices, the country's opening up to the outside world, the welfare system, and regional disparities. The cost of housing, education and other expenditures in people's lives was increasing. The overall level of prices had also risen greatly, but the tax threshold had not been changed, which has substantially increased the tax burden on low-income earners. Second, it was not people-oriented. The tax adjustment mechanism was rigid, and the number of pre-tax deductions and exemptions was unreasonable. The individual income tax system was slow to respond to changes in price levels, lacked a linkage mechanism, and did not fully take into account the taxpayer's support for children and the elderly. Third, it was not conducive to transforming the economic growth model from investment-led to consumption-led. In 2005, consumption alone was obviously not sufficient to promote China's economic growth. The reason was that the distribution system was unreasonable, which reduced people's consumption capacity. Due to the relatively high tax burden, the income level couldn't keep up with the increase in living costs, resulting in a decline in the average propensity to consume (APC) of individuals, while the amount of household savings remained high. Fourth, it was not conducive to the development of China's middle class. A truly modern and stable country must have a bell-shaped structure of the middle-income class as the main body. To maintain the stable, harmonious, sustainable and healthy development of the economy and society, it is crucial to expand the proportion of middle-income earners by raising the income of the low-income group. At the time, the individual income tax system was not conductive to encourage more low-income people to become middle-income earners through legal means.

The problems identified by the Central Committee of the CNDCA coincided with the social needs at that time, and the individual income tax system was in real need of reform.

The Highly Valued CNDCA's Proposal Promotes the Reform

During the two sessions (the annual NPC and CPPCC sessions) in 2005, the Central Committee of the CNDCA submitted a collective proposal on enacting the reform of the individual income tax system. The proposal is based on the principle that individual income tax reform should be given prominence and should play an essential role in regulating social income distribution and narrowing the gap between the rich and the poor. The proposal also contains suggestions on several issues that need attention in the individual income tax reform. First, the standard for deduction of expenses. The proposal is based on the principle that there is a consensus for raising the threshold, which is the most fundamental part and the starting point of the individual income tax reform. The determination of the threshold should take into account the total income and consumption expenditure of residents, the burden coefficient of employees, the tax burden of each income class, the range of price changes, the price comparison index of each region, the rate of economic growth, the international standards and calculation methods, etc. It is necessary to carry out a rational assessment so as to integrate all the above factors. Second, the determination of items eligible for tax deduction and exemption. Relevant deduction and exemption items are formulated according to the individuals' living costs. Taxpayers who need to support the elderly and/or children, or who have unemployed family members, will enjoy tax reduction or remission after approval by the tax department. The individual income tax reform should be people-oriented, optimize the tax rate structure, adjust the tax burden, and give full play to the role of the individual income tax in protecting low-income earners. It should appropriately take care of middle-income earners, and focus on regulating high-income earners. Third, establish a linkage mechanism with price changes. When market prices continue to fluctuate on a large scale, the deduction standards for expenses can be adjusted according to the range of price changes. A relevant linkage mechanism can be established to reduce the impact of market price changes on the living standards of low-income groups and enhance the government's ability to control the economy as a whole.

The proposal from the Central Committee of the CNDCA received a positive reaction from the Ministry of Finance. After carefully studying the content of the proposal, the Ministry of Finance replied, "[The proposal] has put forward many valuable suggestions, which we will study and learn from in individual income tax reform." The reply focuses on several issues: one is in relation to raising the tax threshold. The reply agrees that with the rapid development of China's economy, the income of urban workers has greatly improved in recent years, but at the same time, with the increase in the consumer price index and the deepening of market-oriented reforms in education, housing, and medical care, urban residents' living costs have also increased accordingly. Therefore, it is necessary to adjust the standard of individual income tax deduction and exemption. The Ministry of Finance and the State Administration of Taxation have been conducting in-depth and detailed research on this issue, and have put forward a plan for appropriate adjustment of the deduction standard. At present, the plan has been approved by the State Council, and will be submitted to the Standing Committee of the NPC to amend the relevant provisions of the Individual Income Tax Law. This time, the adjustment of the exemption amount considers the growth of income and consumption expenditure of urban workers across the country. It will reasonably ease the tax burden for urban residents. The second objective is to reform the individual income tax rate. The Ministry of Finance proposes that the structure of the individual income tax rate is relatively complex. The future tax system reform will be conducive to attracting high-tech management talents and individual investors at home and abroad, and also conducive to a fair tax burden, simplifying the tax system. Based on the nine-level excess progressive tax rate, the highest marginal tax rate is appropriately lowered, the tier gap is adjusted, and the number of progressive stages is reduced. A uniformly applicable progressive tax rate is formulated for comprehensive income while a proportional tax rate is applicable to independent incomes. The third is about increasing the strength of individual income tax's function in regulating the income distribution. In recent years, there has been an increasingly strong demand from society to adjust high income and alleviate the unfair distribution of income. The Ministry of Finance and the State Administration of Taxation have further strengthened the adjustment of individual income tax for high-income industries and individuals. However, the current adjustment and collection and management have not been in place for various reasons, which has affected the effectiveness of individual income tax. In the future, we will further improve the Individual Income Tax Law, implement a comprehensive and classified individual income tax system, and unify and standardize expense deduction standards and tax reduction and exemption policies. We will also standardize and broaden the tax base, plug tax loopholes, and establish a scientific and efficient tax collection and management system to manage taxes according to law, collect all taxes owed, and fully exert the function of individual income tax.

In July of the 2005, the Central Committee of the CNDCA submitted a written proposal on "Accelerating the pace of individual income tax and promoting the construction of a socialist harmonious society" at the 10th meeting of the Standing Committee of the 10th CPPCC National Committee. The proposal pointed out that there were still obvious deficiencies in the design and implementation of China's individual tax system in promoting social fairness: first, from the perspective of social development, the level of the tax threshold did not match economic growth; second, from the perspective of taxpayers, the coverage of taxpayers in the individual tax system deviated from the original intention of the design; third, from the perspective of international comparison, the tax system structure was not sufficiently based on solid principles. In face of those deficiencies, the Central Committee of the CNDCA put forward several suggestions: first, to establish a fair and scientific adjustment mechanism for individual tax standards; second, to seize the opportunity to increase the exemption amount reasonably; third, to accelerate the establishment of a comprehensive and classified individual income tax system; fourth, to guide society to deepen their understanding of individual tax reform.

Appealing to the efforts of all sectors of society including the Central Committee of the CNDCA, in October 2005, the 18th meeting of the Standing Committee of the 10th NPC passed the decision on amending the Individual Income Tax Law, increasing the monthly exemption amount from 800 yuan to 1,600 yuan, and adding the requirement that high-income earners should file tax declaration.

Reform of Individual Income Tax Law Has Been Accelerated

After 2005, with the rapid development of China's national economy and the deepening of various reforms, the Individual Income Tax Law has been continuously adjusted and improved according to the prevailing situations. In June 2007, the Standing Committee of the NPC authorized the State Council to revise the income tax on savings deposits in the Individual Income Tax Law, reducing the applicable tax rate from 20% to 5%; in December 2007, the 31st meeting of the Standing Committee of the 10th NPC passed a decision to increase the income tax deduction for monthly wages and salaries from 1,600 yuan to 2,000 yuan; in 2008, the individual income tax on interest from savings deposits was temporarily exempted; in 2009, the double-salary system tax calculation method was abolished; in June 2011, the 21st meeting of the Standing Committee of the 11th NPC decided to increase the monthly deduction threshold from 2,000 yuan to 3,500 yuan and at the same time, the basic tax rate was revised from 5% to 3%. The nine levels of progressive tax rate were reduced to seven levels. The 15% and 40% tax rates were abolished, and the scope of the two low-level tax rates of 3% and 10% as well as the 45% top-level tax rate were expanded.

In June 2018, the Individual Income Tax Law was submitted to the third meeting of the Standing Committee of the 13th NPC for deliberation, and the Individual Income Tax Law underwent another major reform. For the first time, wages and salaries, labor remuneration, and authors' remuneration and royalties, became subject to the comprehensive tax; the monthly deduction threshold for wages and salaries was increased from 3,500 yuan to 5,000 yuan; children's education expenditure, continuing education expenditure, serious illness medical treatment, housing loan interest and housing rent have been treated as deduction items for the first time. The tax rate structure has been optimized and the lower tax rate range has been expanded.

This reform fully reflects it is necessary to strengthen the role of taxation in regulating income distribution, better reduce the tax burden on low- and middle-income earners, and achieve the goal of "increasing income for low-income people, expanding the size of the middle-income group, and adjusting excessively high incomes" to a certain extent. The tax system reform with the largest structural tax reduction has benefited a large number of people and has received a strong and positive response from the general public. In 2005, some suggestions in the proposal by the Central Committee for the CNDCA were not yet mature, but they have been gradually improved and implemented in the following years. The proposal has promoted the reform. As a political party, the CNDCA has fulfilled its function of participating in and deliberating on governance through the CPPCC.

The pace of reform will not stop, political parties will continue to fulfill their duties and the CPPCC proposals will inevitably play a more critical role in the new era.

(Contributed by the Central Committee of the CNDCA)

Several Proposals on the Construction of the Three Gorges Project

4

PROFILE OF THE PROPOSER

SUN YUEQI (1893–1995), originally named Yu Qi, was born in Shaoxing, Zhejiang Province. In 1950, he joined the Revolutionary Committee of the Chinese Kuomintang (RCCK). After 1949, he served as deputy director of the Planning Bureau of the Central Financial and Economics Commission (CFEC), deputy director of the General Management Office of Kailuan Coal Mine, consultant to the Ministry of Coal Industry, president of China Council for the Promotion of Peaceful Reunification (CCPPR), honorary president of the Western Returned Scholars Association (WRSA), etc. He was a member of the 3rd and 4th Central Committee of the RCCK, vice chairman of the 5th and 6th Central Committee of the RCCK, chairman of the 7th Central Supervisory Committee of the RCCK, and honorary chairman of the 8th Central Committee of the RCCK. He was also a member of the 2nd, 3rd, 4th and 8th CPPCC National Committee, and a member of the Standing Committee of the 5th to 7th CPPCC National Committee.

Mr. Sun Focused on This Issue for 40 Years, and Submitted a Proposal of about 10,000 Characters when He Was 97 Years Old and Performed His Duties for over 10 Years

———

The construction of the Three Gorges Project and the management of the Yangtze River flood are the century-old dreams of the Chinese nation. In June 1894, Mr. Sun Yat-sen mentioned in "*A Letter to Li Hongzhang (governor-general of Zhili [or Chihli, now Hebei] Province)*" to generate electricity with the power of the waterfall, store it with a device, and use it anytime and anywhere. In 1919, he further put forward the grand idea of developing the resource of Three Gorges in *The International Development of China*, "…the rapids should be dammed up to form locks to enable crafts to ascend the river as well as to generate water power." Since the founding of the PRC, Mao Zedong and other Party and state leaders attached great importance to and cared about the feasibility of the Three Gorges Project, and expressed their vision for the construction of the Three Gorges with poems such as

> "*(To hold back clouds and rains o'er Mount Witch's crest)*
> *Until between steep cliffs emerges a placid lake.*
> *Mount Goddess standing still as before*
> *Would be surprised to find no more*
> *The world of yore.*"[1]

———

1. Translated by Xu Yuanchong.

As the largest water conservancy project in the world today, the Three Gorges Project has witnessed various controversies since it was first proposed because of its profound impacts on the national economy and people's livelihoods. There are many supporters, and not a few opposing voices. Someone asked who made the greatest contribution to the Three Gorges Project, and Pan Jiazheng, a famous water conservancy engineer, once replied, "Those who oppose the Three Gorges Project make the greatest contribution to it." Zhang Chaoran, the chief engineer of the Three Gorges Project, also said, "These objections are also very beneficial to the construction of the Three Gorges Project. They allow us to pay more attention to scientific demonstration and thus make the project perfect. Different opinions about the construction of major projects should be heard, and many opinions have been fully considered in constructing the Three Gorges Project." In this way, with the problems raised by the objectors overcome, the project's quality was guaranteed.

As a member of the Standing Committee of the 5th to 7th National Committee of the CPPCC, a member of the 2nd, 3rd, 4th and 8th National Committee of the CPPCC, a member of the 3rd and 4th Central Committee of the RCCK, vice chairman of the 5th and 6th Central Committee of the RCCK, chairman of the 7th Central Supervisory Committee of the RCCK, and honorary chairman of the 8th Central Committee of the RCCK, Sun Yueqi was one of those who explicitly raised objections. His in-depth and detailed arguments ensured that the Three Gorges Project avoided many potential mistakes and problems, and gradually improved its construction. Additionally, how he expressed his opinions reflected the characteristics and advantages of China's socialist consultative democracy system.

The Beginning

Sun Yueqi had a deep connection with the Three Gorges Project. As early as the 1920s, he was determined to save the country through developing industry. Facing difficult internal and external troubles, he participated in and presided over the establishment of the Muling Coal Mine, Zhongfu Coal Mine, Yumen Oil Mine and other oil and coal companies in Heilongjiang, Liaoning, Henan and other places. These oil and coal companies laid the cornerstone for the development of China's heavy industry, and he was known as "a leading scholar in industry and mining." In May 1946, the Kuomintang National Resources Commission of the Ministry of Economic Affairs (referred to as the "Resources Commission") was separated from the Kuomintang National Government's Ministry of Economic Affairs. It became the "ministerial-level unit" in charge of state-owned enterprises at that time, with Sun Yueqi as the deputy chairman. In May 1948, Sun Yueqi was promoted to chairman of the Resource Committee and became the head of this huge department.

In the 1940s, as one of the important institutions directly in charge of China's water conservancy undertakings, the Resources Commission did a lot of preparatory work to develop the Three Gorges. The Commission specially employed John Lucian Savage, a world-renowned expert in dam engineering and one of the founders of the U.S. Bureau of Reclamation's Engineering and Research Center, as a consultant. He visited the Three Gorges twice and compiled the "Preliminary Report on the Three Gorges Project on the Yangtze River." Sun Yueqi also participated in related work. According to Sun: "He (referring to Savage) is a world-class expert who designed 60 dams, and he chose Nanjinguan as the site for the Three Gorges Dam. At that time, the Resources Commission sent 52 people to participate in the design, and of course, I agreed with it." But just as the Three Gorges Project design entered a critical stage, the Kuomintang government was saddled with substantial military expenditures due to the civil war, and the national economy was almost on the brink of collapse. The Kuomintang National Government thus promulgated economic emergency measures, "for work that will not see results in a short time, the funding needs to be suspended or postponed." Obviously, the Three Gorges Project falls into this category. In May 1947, the Kuomintang Resource Committee announced that "the Three Gorges Project has been suspended," and Sun Yueqi's first involvement with the Three Gorges Project also stopped.

His Involvement Continued

After the PRC was founded, the development and governance of the entire Yangtze River Basin became a major concern for the CPC Central Committee and the State Council. They established the Yangtze River Water Conservancy

Commission, an agency for the governance of the entire basin, and invited the Soviet government to send experts to China to assist in the planning of the Yangtze River Basin and the design of the Three Gorges Project. In the 1980s, the construction of the Three Gorges Project, an essential super-large project in national economic construction, became a hot issue for Chinese people. To build or not to build? Which were more important, short-term gains or long-term development? Should there be a low dam or a high dam? The related questions became a topic of discussion in the streets.

In 1980, under the leadership of the State Planning Commission and the State Science and Technology Commission, the demonstration of the Three Gorges Project began. Sun Yueqi, who survived the Tangshan earthquake, was elected as a member of the Standing Committee at the Third Session of the 5th CPPCC National Committee. He and many members of the CPPCC focused on the issue of the construction of the Three Gorges Project.

Brave Enough to Put Forward Radical Suggestions

On April 5, 1984, the State Council approved the "Report on the Review Opinions on the Feasibility Study Report of the Three Gorges Project of the Yangtze River" submitted by the State Planning Commission, and proposed that the main project be officially started in 1986. Subsequently, the State Council established a preparatory group for the Three Gorges Project, and the Three Gorges Project on the Yangtze River would be launched soon. Yet at this time, among the members of the CPPCC National Committee, a proposal for delaying the Three Gorges Dam project was being prepared. Sun Yueqi, the then vice-chairman of the Central Committee of the RCCK, also a member of the Standing Committee of the CPPCC National Committee and head of the Economic Construction Group of the CPPCC, boldly submitted a letter to express his doubts based on what he knew and on the opinions of some experts. Huang Liangchen, a member of the 6th and 7th Standing Committee of the CPPCC National Committee, and a member of the 2nd to 5th National Committee, wrote an article recalling the situation at that time: "Because the 'Cultural Revolution' only ended not long ago, everyone had lingering fears. But

Mr. Sun (Sun Yueqi) took the lead in signing the proposal, which set an example for other members. And I also signed. Although Mr. Sun experienced ups and downs over the years, he still shoulders the responsibility for the country and the people, rather than considering his personal gains and losses."

During the Third Session of the 6th CPPCC National Committee held from March 25 to April 8, 1985, 167 members of the CPPCC National Committee put forward 17 proposals individually or jointly on the Three Gorges Project, suggesting that it should be postponed. Thus the Economic Construction Group of the CPPCC National Committee set up an investigation group headed by Sun Yueqi to handle the comprehensive management of the Yangtze River Basin and for the construction of the Three Gorges Project, and organized experts from various fields to go to the middle reaches of the Yangtze River for further investigation and research. On May 30, 92-year-old Sun Yueqi led an investigation team consisting of ten people, including Lin Hua, former deputy director of the State Planning Commission; Xu Chi, former adviser to the State Economic Commission; and Wang Xingrang, the former deputy minister of the Ministry of Commerce, travelling from Beijing to Chengdu. They surveyed Dujiangyan and the upper reaches of the Minjiang River near Chengdu, took a ship along the Three Gorges Reservoir area to Wanxian, Baxian, and Zigui via Chongqing to learn about reservoir inundation and resettlement issues, and then inspected the Sandouping Three Gorges Dam site by ship. They passed through the Gezhouba Ship Lock to Yichang, then traveled via Jingzhou and Shashi to the Jingjiang River Embankment by car. They checked the dangerous Yanka section, which faces the major current; they then went directly to Wuchang. During their 38-day research activities, in spite of the heat, they not only took on-site inspections, but also held more than 40 symposiums with experts from various fields and local Party and government leaders to listen to their opinions and learn about the history and current situation in relation to transportation, water conservancy, electricity, earthquakes, meteorology and hydrology. During the daytime, the investigation team would conduct investigations or hold symposiums; at night, they would conduct analysis and research and write investigation materials. Sun Yueqi had a very good memory, and sometimes he did not need a notebook—his brain recorded many data.

Members of the CPPCC National Committee made field visits to the construction site of the Three Gorges Hydro Project and made many suggestions and proposals.

After returning to Beijing, the investigation team sorted and analyzed the materials obtained from the investigation despite the exhaustion of the journey and the sweltering heat of midsummer. Sun Yueqi also presided over many meetings to discuss research and write reports. Based on the results of this investigation, he raised different opinions on the launch of the Three Gorges Project. He advocated that the water conservancy development in the Yangtze River Basin should start from upstream, rather than rushing to build the Three Gorges Project, and he led the investigation team to write reports jointly with more than 10,000 characters. With investigations of the history of water control at home and abroad, the report pointed out that there were problems in the design of the Three Gorges Project and the estimated budget of the Three Gorges Project may lead to inflation, and thus suggests the combination of renovation and dredging with efforts put explicitly put into the latter. Related experience from the US and Germany can be referred to. Hydropower development must tackle easy problems first, and then difficult ones, and the Project should be developed progressively on each tributary of the Yangtze River. In addition, six special reports on investment, flood control, navigation, power generation, and other issues are attached to the major one. At the end of July, 1985, the investigation team sent this investigation report to the CPPCC National Committee in the name of the Economic Construction Group of the CPPCC National Committee, entitled "Three Gorges Project Cannot Be Launched Recently," which received high regards. Yang Jingren, then the first vice chairman of the CPPCC National Committee, held a banquet at the United Front Work Department of the CPC Central Committee to express appreciation to Sun Yueqi and members of the investigation team. Deng Yingchao, the then chairwoman of the CPPCC National Committee, met with Sun Yueqi and sent her regards to him.

A Close Friend of the CPC

The opinions of Sun Yueqi and the Yangtze River Basin Comprehensive Management and Three Gorges Project Investigation Group of the CPPCC National Committee attracted great attention from the Party and the State. In June 1986, the Central Committee of the CPC and the State Council issued the "Notice on Issues Concerning the Demonstration Work of the Three Gorges Project," instructing the Ministry of Water Conservancy and Electric Power, which was in charge of the Three Gorges Project, to organize a broader demonstration, re-submit a feasibility report, and send it to the State Council for review. At the same time, the Preparatory Group was replaced by the Three Gorges Regional Economic Development Office. The Ministry of Water Conservancy and Electric Power also immediately set up a leading group to demonstrate the Three Gorges Project.

In order to show the importance attached to the opinions and suggestions of the CPPCC, Cheng Zihua, vice chairman of the 6th CPPCC National Committee, joined the leading group of the Three Gorges Project demonstration. Sun Yueqi was appointed the consultant of the leading group. At the same time, the Review Committee for the Three Gorges Project was established to further demonstrate the feasibility of the Project.

Under the auspices of the Ministry of Water Conservancy and Electric Power, 14 expert groups were established around the main issues of the dispute. Among the 412 members of the expert groups and consultants of the leading group, there were more than 20 members from the CPPCC National Committee. By the time the NPC passed the resolution on the construction of the Three Gorges Project, more than 50 members of the CPPCC National Committee had participated in this work. During the discussion for more than eight months, debates had never been so intense in New China's decision-making history. In particular, the opinions and criticisms of some members of the CPPCC National Committee were quite thought-provoking.

Sun Yueqi wrote a number of reports, stating his opinions and suggestions in a clear and direct manner at the CPPCC meeting and the discussion meeting held by the State Council. In July 1986, Sun Yueqi put forward the report "The Demonstration of the Three Gorges Project Should Make Comparison Between Two Schemes of the Construction: Faster or Slower" in the name of the Yangtze River Basin Comprehensive Management and the Three Gorges Project Investigation Team of the Economic Construction Group of the CPPCC National Committee. The CPPCC submitted the report to the Central Committee of the CPC, and one month later this report became one of the important reference documents for the second (expanded) meeting of the Three Gorges Project Demonstration Leading Group of the Ministry of Water Conservancy and Electric Power.

In December of the same year, at the third (expanded) meeting of the Three Gorges Project Demonstration Leading Group of the Ministry of Water Conservancy and Electric Power, Sun Yueqi wrote a speech of more than 16,000 words, which was read by the secretary of the CPPCC due to Sun Yueqi's advanced age. After listening to the report of the flood control expert group at the meeting, he made some comments. He said that "the basic principles of planning for the Yangtze River Basin should be unified planning, comprehensive development, appropriate division of labor, and phased implementation." Although the Three Gorges Project "has the largest scale, the longest construction period, and the largest budget, and is one of the most important projects in the development of the Yangtze River, it does not mean that it should be launched immediately; instead, it should depend on 'whether the conditions are ripe.'" He also pointed out: First, on the issue of flood control, it was necessary to prevent the thought of waiting for the Three Gorges Project and thinking everything will be fine after the Three Gorges Project. Second, the development of electric power requires a combination of hydroelectric and thermal power, and measures should be taken according to local conditions. The development of hydroelectric power in the Yangtze River Basin should be done first with tributaries and then with the main stream. Third, shipping rather than flood control should be given priority on the Chuanjiang River. Given the remaining sediments, clearing waterways comes first. Under the guidance of seeking truth from facts, referring to national conditions, and putting the easy before the difficult, Sun also pointed out that flood control, power generation and shipping were urgent tasks to deal with if China wanted to achieve the grand goal of quadrupling the total industrial and agricultural output value by the end of the 20th century. At the end of his speech, Sun Yueqi said earnestly that as a member of the CPPCC National Committee, "in line with the principle of 'long-term coexistence, mutual supervision, sincerity, and sharing weal and woe,' and in response to the call of 'informed efforts' to strive to be a true friend of the CPC, I, a 93-year-old man, with a pure heart, expressed myself frankly, and sincerely welcomed criticism if I've said anything inappropriate."

Put Forward Suggestions Based on Investigations

After in-depth researches, in November 1987, Sun Yueqi wrote a report of nearly 20,000 characters. In the report titled "The Basic Principles of Planning for the Yangtze River Basin Should Be Unified Planning, Comprehensive Development, Appropriate Division of Labor, and Phased Implementation," he seriously pointed out that we should learn from the two lessons in history (to save the North at the expense of the South and to use low-lying land around the river for flood storage and agriculture alternatively), avoid "saving the lower reaches at the expense of the upper reaches," speed up the completion of flood control projects in the plains, remove river barriers in accordance with the law, conscientiously eliminate hidden dangers of the Jingjiang Embankment, and resolutely correct the wrong practice of "using low-lying land around the river for flood storage and agriculture alternatively," and also actively manage the problem regarding Dongting Lake and speed up the construction of tributary reservoirs. In 1988, on the commemoration of the 90th anniversary of the birth of late Premier Zhou Enlai, he carefully studied Zhou Enlai's expositions on the comprehensive management of the Yangtze River Basin and the Three Gorges and exchanged ideas with Tian Fang, former deputy director of the Economic Research Institute of the State Planning Commission. Later, he published "Learning from Zhou Enlai's Glorious Teachings on Governing the Yangtze and Yellow Rivers" in the *Tuanjie Bao (Unity)*, proposing that "The Three Gorges Project is a long-term development goal, and a very cautious attitude is needed in building it." He wrote that overall planning for the entire Yangtze River Basin should be carried out before constructing the Three Gorges Project. He also summed up views on the Three Gorges Project from the 1960s and 1970s. He pointed out that we should learn from the lessons of the Yellow River planning and the Sanmenxia Project, learn from the criticism of the Gezhouba Project, and avoid making decisions in a rush.

On March 6, 1989, when the Three Gorges Project Demonstration Leading Group met to deliberate on the feasibility report of the Three Gorges Project, Sun Yueqi made a speech. More than ten days later, on March 21, at the Second Session of the 7th CPPCC National Committee, 13 members of the CPPCC

Beautiful Three Gorges

National Committee, including Sun Yueqi and Lin Hua, made a joint speech. In response to the "Three Gorges Hydro Project Feasibility Report" reviewed by Ministry of Water Conservancy and Electric Power and the Ministry of Energy and reformulated by the Yangtze River Planning Office in February, they again voiced comments and suggestions, and presented a written conference statement of about 29,000 characters, entitled "Talking about the Three Gorges."

In March 1990, during the Third Session of the 7th CPPCC National Committee, Sun Yueqi supplemented and revised his previous statement in "Talking about the Three Gorges," and once again submitted a written speech of about 40,000 characters, entitled "On the Comprehensive Management of the Yangtze River Basin and the Three Gorges Project." In it he introduced in detail the previous investigations of and researches on the Three Gorges Project, systematically summarized his previous research results and insights on the comprehensive management of the Yangtze River Basin and the Three Gorges Project, and gave suggestions on five aspects of the project: flood control, power generation, shipping, South-to-North Water Diversion, and the ecological environment.

In July 1990, the State Council held a report meeting on demonstrating the Three Gorges Project in Beijing. Premier Li Peng listened to the report of the leading group on the demonstration and the new feasibility report. The 97-year-old Sun Yueqi attended the meeting, made a remarkable speech, and submitted a 48,000-character letter. In the letter, he synthesized the opinions from the demonstrations and experts in the Three Gorges and the water conservancy, energy, ecological environment, geology, and other aspects of Sichuan and the Yangtze River Basin. Opinions of other experts, including those from the World Bank, were also considered. The Three Gorges Project Leading Group adopted many constructive comments and suggestions, which contributed to the smooth construction of the Three Gorges Project.

On April 3, 1992, after research, design, and planning for half a century, the Fifth Session of the 7th National People's Congress passed the resolution "On the Construction of the Three Gorges Project on the Yangtze River" with 1,767 votes in favor, 177 votes against, 664 abstentions, 25 absences. In addition, based on the review report by the Financial and Economic Affairs Committee of the NPC, the Congress decided to list the construction of the Three Gorges Project in the ten-year plan for national economic and social development. Since then, the Three Gorges Project has moved from demonstration to implementation.

During the demonstration of the Three Gorges Project, Sun Yueqi, with his high sense of responsibility, made great efforts for the demonstration of the Three Gorges Project despite his age. His sincere attitude and patriotism have been highly praised by the Party and government leaders, who have called him "a close friend of the CPC."

(Contributed by the Central Committee of the RCCK)

No. 2305, the Second Session of the 12th CPPCC National Committee to the Second Session of the 13th CPPCC National Committee

Several Proposals to Vigorously Implement Targeted Poverty Alleviation

5

PROFILE OF THE PROPOSER

Li Bin, born in March 1962 in Taixing, Jiangsu Province, is a member of the Jiusan Society, starting his career in August 1983. He graduated from the Chinese Academy of Geological Sciences (CAGS) with an in-work postgraduate degree, majoring in geological engineering, and hold the titles of doctor of engineering and researcher. He was a member of the 11th to 13th CPPCC National Committee. He is a member of the Standing Committee of the Central Committee of the Jiusan Society, chairman of Guangxi Zhuang Autonomous Region Committee of the Jiusan Society, and vice chairman of the People's Government of Guangxi Zhuang Autonomous Region.

Working Together to Overcome Hardship

————

After the 18th National Congress of the CPC, the world's most extensive poverty eradication campaign was launched in China. General Secretary Xi Jinping pointed out that "no one should be left behind when building a well-off society in all respects; no one should be left behind on the way to shared prosperity." China has achieved remarkable results after more than seven years of targeted poverty alleviation, particularly after more than four years of the battle against poverty. The intensity, scale and achievements of China's poverty alleviation campaign are unprecedented in the world. This ancient oriental country has written the story of the most successful poverty alleviation in the history of human social development.

After the battle against poverty began, the majority of CPPCC members and the CPPCC political parties and people's groups have taken actions on the front-line to help the poor. Some have actively carried out grass-roots research, some have organized donations, and some have summarized their suggestions into proposals and put them forward at the CPPCC. Since the Second Session of the 12th CPPCC in 2014, 270 proposals have been put forward around targeted poverty alleviation and for winning the battle against poverty. With a variety of measures, the proposals all played positive roles in this great cause, helping promote the implementation of poverty alleviation strategy, enriching the scientific planning of poverty alleviation in the "Thirteenth Five-Year Plan" period, and making sure the result could be achieved as scheduled.

On November 7, 2019, the Ninth Meeting of the Standing Committee of the 13th CPPCC National Committee honored 100 most influential CPPCC proposals in 70 years since the founding of the CPPCC. Among them, "Proposals to Vigorously Implement Targeted Poverty Alleviation" was a group proposals focusing on targeted poverty alleviation, submitted by 419 CPPCC National Committee members including Li Bin, as well as the Central Committee of political parties, the ACFIC, and the circles of education.

Li Bin, a Member of the CPPCC National Committee:
No Speeches without Prior Research

Li Bin, living in the city of Guilin, is a member of the CPPCC National Committee, vice chairman of the Guangxi Zhuang Autonomous Region and chairman of the Guangxi Committee of the Jiusan Society. His proposal "Innovative Mechanisms to Implement Targeted Poverty Alleviation Management," which he submitted at the Second Session of the 12th CPPCC National Committee in 2014, is listed among the 100 most influential proposals.

In his research, Li Bin found that while poverty alleviation work made remarkable achievements over the years, there were still certain problems as

On October 31, 2015, Li Bin researched on precise poverty alleviation in the targeted poverty-stricken village of Chengxiang Town, Longan County.

the target, scale and distribution of poverty alleviation work had changed. For example, the design of the poverty alleviation system overemphasized on the comprehensive expansion of poverty alleviation work, ignoring the fact that the work should be done progressively with consideration of specific "targets." In terms of the support distribution mechanism, the poorer the regions were, the larger the support they received, the more poverty alleviation projects were actioned, and the more matching funds[1] shall be raised in poor areas, which undoubtedly increased the economic pressure of local departments and people. Due to the large scale and severity of poverty in some areas and the weakness of local finance, the outstanding contradiction between support and demand couldn't be reconciled. Many poverty alleviation projects were "aborted" or "shelved" due to the difficulty of obtaining enough funds, and some projects ended up "Jerry-built" or "unfinished" projects.

Li Bin also commented on the poverty alleviation assessment and evaluation mechanism at the time. In his opinion, poverty alleviation assessment was too biased toward certain indicators such as gross regional product and farmers' annual per capita income growth. This led to the misunderstanding of poverty alleviation work as using poverty alleviation funds to create "model" sites to pursue political achievements. The following problems began to emerge: rushing for quick success and mindlessly going ahead with industrial projects; the waste caused by each department going its own way without communicating with other ones when implementing poverty alleviation programs; faking the statistical data on poverty alleviation results to pretend that objectives have been "met." These lead to the false assessments of the effectiveness of poverty alleviation performance, hidden poverty, etc. In addition, the "universal poverty alleviation" and "inclusive poverty alleviation" mechanism has undermined the role of farmers as the main actors of this project.

According to his practical research, Li Bin submitted the proposal "An Innovative Mechanism to Implement Targeted Poverty Alleviation Management" at the Second Session of the 12th CPPCC National Committee in March 2014.

---

1. In China's new financial management system, many economic projects have their funds constituted by two parts: those allocated by national or local authorities, and those raised by the institutions that apply for the projects. The latter is usually referred to as "matching funds."

The proposal not only listed the problems found during the research, but also elaborated on the solutions, such as expanding the targets from "impoverished counties" to larger regions, coordinating development between urban and rural areas, accelerating industrialization and urbanization, support agriculture with industry, and alleviating poverty through developing industries, and sparing no effort in registering poor households and in building poverty alleviation project libraries...

After being submitted, the proposal was highly praised and fully adopted by the Poverty Relief Office under the State Council, and the relevant suggestions were absorbed and implemented into the practical work of China's strategy to promote targeted poverty alleviation and poverty eradication.

For Li Bin, doing research on the front line of poverty alleviation is his daily work, and this allows him to keep an active mind, to keep in touch with the actual problems, and to think about measures to be taken.

"Each rural village stricken by poverty is different and has its own characteristics. Take Guangxi as an example—people in some villages have certain skills. Still, the natural or production conditions are poor, and the lack of water or soil makes it unsuitable for growing crops, so their skills have nowhere to use. Some places have good natural conditions, but local authorities would rather sit and wait rather than seek change. Their knowledge and ability cannot adapt to the need of production development." Li Bin believes poverty alleviation work should be closely integrated with ongoing urbanization and agricultural modernization. The villages stricken with deep poverty and poor living conditions should be reclassified into different categories and relocated to other places in stages to maximize the effects of poverty alleviation funds, so that children in poor mountainous areas can receive a good education and change their lives.

"No speeches without prior research" has become a necessary quality for a qualified CPPCC member. In addition to Li Bin's proposal, the following proposals concerning targeted poverty alleviation are also listed as influential proposals: "The Proposal for Targeted Poverty Alleviation to Ensure the Simultaneous Realization of Prosperity in Minority Areas" by Niu Ruji, a member of the China Association for Promoting Democracy (CAPD); "The Proposal for 'High-quality Poverty Alleviation' to Help 'Targeted Poverty Alleviation' and the 'Culturally Well-off' to Serve the 'Overall Well-off'" by Wu Weishan, a member from the circles of culture and art; "The Proposal for Encouraging the Cultivation of Traditional Chinese Medicine in Poor Rural Areas to Help Targeted Poverty Alleviation" by An A-yue, a member of the ethnic minorities circles. Each proposal has a story behind, and what they have in common is that the proposals all emerge from what the proposers have seen and what they have learned from their visits and researches. This illustrates that for a proposal to be valid, it must be down to earth.

Proposal of the Education Circles: Acquiring Knowledge and Skills before Poverty Alleviation

On September 9, 2015, the 31st Teachers' Day, General Secretary Xi Jinping wrote to all teachers participating in the Guizhou Workshop by Beijing Normal University in the "National Training Program (2014)," pointing out that "A prerequisite of poverty alleviation is to help people acquire necessary knowledge and skills. Ensuring that children in poor areas receive a good education is an important task of development-driven poverty alleviation, and an important way of cutting off the intergenerational transmission of poverty." Taking education as a priority task in poverty alleviation can fundamentally improve the rural population's quality and lay a solid foundation for building a moderately prosperous society in all respects.

During the Fourth Session of the 12th CPPCC National Committee, members of the education circles submitted "A Proposal on the Implementation of Education Information Technology in Targeted Poverty Alleviation Projects." It pointed out that education policy in relation to poverty alleviation should focus on elementary education in rural areas, with targeted measures implemented in different places, especially in central and Western China where elementary education is still weak. Students and teachers flow into towns and cities, which renders the lack of rural education resources and excellent teachers.

This phenomenon has been repeatedly reported in the media. For example, a reporter from "The Education Weekly" by *CPPCC Daily* once mentioned such a dilemma in the article "Reducing the Class Size and Improving Teaching Quality in the Liangshan Region." According to this article in 2017, some members of the CPPCC National Committee went to Liangshan Yi Autonomous Prefecture in Sichuan for research, and saw that the classes in a local school usually had around 80 students each—there was even one with 120 children. In a middle school, there was no toilet in a dormitory building. The winter night was freezing, and the children had to go to a distant latrine in pairs, which was very unsafe...

The proposal highlights three main issues: first, the problem of "incomplete, insufficient classes and poor lessons" in rural schools; second, the low professional level of teachers; and third, the high proportion of children left behind. In response to these problems, the proposal put forward suggestions under six headings: building integrated "digital schools" in urban and rural areas, improving rural teachers' computer literacy, promoting joint efforts from all sides, building a precise database for education poverty alleviation, increasing financial investment, and establishing a strong and sound system for education in these areas. Each suggestion also had several related specific measures.

The implementation of this proposal was directed by the Ministry of Education and co-directed by the Ministry of Finance. In a letter responding to the proposal, the Ministry of Education responded to the education circles' concerns and said that in recent years, the Ministry of Education had adhered to the core concept of promoting the deep integration of information technology into teaching, followed the two basic guidelines of practice-driven and mechanism innovation, and accelerated the development of information technology for education.

On February 2, 2016, the General Office of the Ministry of Education issued the "Highlights of Education Informatization Work in 2016." In the section of "Accelerating the 'School Access of Broadband Network' in Primary and Secondary Schools," it promotes the incorporation of information technology infrastructure into school construction standards and basic school conditions. Combined with strategies of targeted poverty alleviation , the Internet access in poor villages and weak schools shall be promoted, so as to achieve an Internet access rate of 95% in primary and secondary schools. The Office urges the work of "comprehensively improving the basic conditions of compulsory education in schools in poor areas" in various regions, ensuring information technology investment in rural schools, with the goal that the country's primary and secondary schools should have multimedia teaching resources—the proportion of ordinary classrooms equipped with multimedia teaching equipment in primary and secondary schools should reach 80% and 50% respectively.

Education is a major matter of people's livelihoods. Improving education is essential to development-driven poverty alleviation and an important way to fundamentally lift people out of poverty. The members and project contractors agreed that the development of information technology, such as the Internet, cloud computing and big data, has brought about changes in the concept of education, in the modes of education and in the ways of learning, which has given rise to a new educational environment and provided new possibilities for poverty alleviation in the education realm. Education information technology has great potential, which is the focus of many visionary members because it can benefit people's livelihoods.

The Central Committees of the Political Parties and the ACFIC: Aiming at the Weak Links and Making Targeted Efforts

In June 2016, the State Council Leading Group Office of Poverty Alleviation and Development invited the central committees of eight political parties to carry out democratic supervision over the implementation of major poverty-alleviation policies and measures, and the use of funds for the impoverished in Western and Central provinces and regions with a high incidence of poverty. This is a major decision made by the Central Committee of the CPC with General Secretary Xi Jinping at its core, and is an institutional arrangement to bring into play the advantages of democratic supervision to promote the implementation of poverty elimination policies.

In accordance with the unified deployment of the United Front Work Department of the Central Committee of the CPC, the central committees of the eight political parties were paired with the eight poor provinces or regions. They immediately carried out full-scale democratic supervision over poverty elimination work. Led by the main leaders of the political parties' central committees, the members went deep into the poorest mountain villages and households to listen to their opinions, so as to understand more accurately the actual situation of the current work of targeted poverty alleviation and elimination. While effectively carrying out this democratic supervision, the parties could also have a closer look at the implementation of this great project.

Since then, the Central Committee of each political party and the ACFIC have submitted many proposals around specific aspects of poverty alleviation based on their own areas of strength.

First, the industrial and financial fields.

Among the 33 proposals submitted by the Revolutionary Committee of the Chinese KMT to the Fifth Session of the 12th CPPCC National Committee, three were related to poverty alleviation and elimination, among which the proposal on further promoting financing targeted poverty alleviation was in the first place. All-around measures of targeted poverty alleviation in the financing realm were proposed. The proposals suggested that those measures shall be integrated with the development of industries by strengthening industrial cultivation; financial innovation shall be promoted to enhance the effectiveness of the measures; and the functions of capital markets and insurance shall be better utilized to enhance the measures' depth and breadth. It also proposed improving the county-level financial service system to enhance the measures' efficiency and proficiency and strengthening risk prevention to ensure the measures' safe operation.

Based on their research, the Central Committee of the China National Democratic Construction Association also put forward proposals for carrying out in-depth targeted poverty alleviation and elimination policies, increasing financial support for targeted poverty alleviation, etc. In addition, it put forward proposals focusing on the rehabilitation treatment for rural children with disabilities to achieve in-depth implementation of targeted poverty alleviation policies.

Poverty alleviation through industrial development has been the main focus and battlefield of the national "Ten Thousand Enterprises Help Ten Thousand Villages" campaign. Since 2016, the ACFIC has started the "Ten Thousand Enterprises Help Ten Thousand Villages" action, bringing a large number of resources to poor areas. These experiences have been transformed into proposals of great importance, such as the "Proposal on Supporting the Development of Specialty Industries to Enhance the Endogenous Power of Poverty Alleviation in Border Ethnic Areas" and the "Proposal on Making Private Enterprises More Responsible for Poverty Alleviation" in 2019.

Second, the education field.

There are many cases of poverty alleviation through vocational training. For example, in Dongxiang, Gansu, three months of training in making Lanzhou hand-pulled noodles can double a person's income; Beijing Changping Vocational School explored the "school-town-village" cooperation model, holding "spring cake banquets" in village of Kangling, which has enabled the village to increase its tourism income from 30,000 yuan in 2005 to 10 million yuan today, thus attracting and retaining young people to the village through industry, and helping to revitalize the countryside.

The Central Committee of CAPD, which has a large number of experts and talented people in the field of education, pointed out in its "Proposal on Vigorously Developing Secondary Vocational Education and Helping Rural Areas to Fight Poverty" that secondary vocational education is the type of education closest to the rural disadvantaged and the working class, and can directly improve their employability and income level. The proposal suggests that the state should start the implementation of the "National Project on Poverty Alleviation through Secondary Vocational Education" as soon as possible, and "secondary education for poverty eradication" should be explicitly listed as one of the "priorities." Implementing the "Plan to Improve the Capacity of Secondary Vocational Education in Concentrated and Contiguous Poor Areas" should pay special attention to secondary vocational education in developing nation-wide high school education, particularly supporting the cultivation of school characteristics and its ability to serve local industrial development. City and county governments should be encouraged to financially support various entities to provide education and training services. The proposal also suggests encouraging developed regions to help with the secondary vocational education in less developed ares, removing policy barriers, relaxing enrollment restrictions, expanding the scale of enrollment in poor areas, and promoting targeted enrollment toward registered low-income families.

Third, strong mechanisms for delivery.

In its "Proposal on Innovative and Targeted Poverty Alleviation Mechanism to Ensure Long-term Poverty Elimination," the Central Committee of the Jiusan Society specially analyzed the problems in the existing poverty alleviation mechanism, including the use of resources, the "hollowing out" phenomenon, the targeted poverty households, the subsistence allowance scheme, the assessment system and low-level poverty elimination. The proposal suggests exploring modes of assistance based on the construction of central villages, exploring the poverty alleviation mechanism with resources sent to villages and help given to households, improving the assessment mechanism of poverty elimination, and specifying the classification of poverty, etc.

Rural subsistence allowances are a problematic area in the subsistence allowance scheme. The Central Committee of China Zhi Gong Party (CZGP) has noticed that the implementation of the current subsistence allowance scheme in rural areas is prone to "abuse" and "variation," resulting in problems such as giving allowances based on social relationships. In this regard, the Central Committee of CZGP has submitted the "Proposal on Accelerating the Development of a Control System for the Income Standards of Rural Subsistence Allowances to Promote Targeted Poverty Alleviation." It is proposed that an easy-to-operate system of indicators should be established as soon as possible for evaluating the economic status and related issues; a special assessment body should be set up; a mechanism to promote inter-departmental work should be instituted to ensure fair and just implementation and proactive supervision over the subsistence allowance scheme; and at the same time, applicants who refuse to report, or conceal their family's financial status, and those who do not meet the requirements of the declaration, should be subjected to investigation and punishment.

Fourth, the medical field.

Disease is an essential factor in causing poverty and in causing people to fall back into poverty. Although the majority of impoverished people are enrolled in the new rural cooperative medical care system or the basic medical insurance system for non-working urban residents, the coverage of medical insurance payments is limited, and many medical expenses are not covered. Once a family member has "catastrophic medical expenses" or large medical expenses due to certain diseases, the family will face a serious financial burden and is likely to be reduced to a low-income or poor family. In Guangxi, for example, the prevalence of thalassemia is 14.95%, which directly leads to a much higher birth defects ratio than the national level, and many families fall into poverty as a result.

The Central Committee of the Chinese Peasants and Workers Democratic Party (CPWDP), which has the advantage in medicine and health, is also paying attention to this issue. The "Proposal on Closely Following the Role of Health Poverty Alleviation in Targeted Poverty Alleviation," is concerned with health poverty alleviation in ethnic areas. The proposal suggests that efforts should be made to accelerate infrastructure construction in these areas, reduce travel and logistics costs and increase access to information, strengthen education and training to enhance self-development capacity, improve the new medical and health system and implement health poverty alleviation projects, continuously increase support for special industries, and support ethnic areas in developing specific industries on an appropriate scale.

Fifth, other issues.

No matter how hard it is, children's growth should be supported. At present, malnutrition among children and adolescents in poor areas of China still exists. The nutritional status of children and adolescents in poor western villages is still at a low level compared with other developing countries. The support for nutritious lunches for rural compulsory education students is low, and nutrition education and food safety supervision in poor areas are weak.

The Central Committee of China Democratic League (CDL) pointed out in its "Proposal on Strengthening Nutrition for Children and Youth in Poverty and Reducing the Health Disparity between Urban and Rural Areas" that the concept of "poverty alleviation in nutrition" should be established, and a separate project should be launched to help those nutritionally poor children and youth in poverty-stricken areas. The proposal also suggests formulating an inclusive policy on "nutritious school meals" for poverty-stricken areas, setting up a "model base for school canteens," creating a "training program for school nutritionists," establishing a nutrition guidance system for primary and secondary schools, working out a "poverty alleviation program in nutrition for families" and setting up a mechanism for tracking and evaluating the nutrition and health status of students.

The Central Committee of CZGP, which works with overseas Chinese, is concerned about the returned overseas Chinese family members with financial difficulties, especially those from overseas Chinese agricultural farms and forestry farms. The Central Committee of CZGP suggested in its "Proposal on Including Poor Returned Overseas Chinese Dependents from Chinese Agriculture and Forestry Farms in Targeted Poverty Alleviation" that the overall design of the project should be improved as soon as possible to include poor returned overseas Chinese dependents from Chinese agriculture and forestry farms in targeted poverty alleviation work, to conduct surveys and mapping of their situation, to register the poor households, to establish and improve the mechanism for helping them, and to help them solve their difficulties, to promote poverty alleviation and increase their income according to local conditions and in a targeted way.

Social assistance is an essential part of China's security system, playing the role of the bottom line and dealing with emergencies. The Central Committee of the Taiwan Democratic Self-government League (TDSL) learned from its research in Chongqing that among more than 1.6 million poverty alleviation targets in the city, 240,000 poverty alleviation targets are included in the scope of the rural subsistence allowances underwriting scheme. In 2017, the city spent 2.151 billion yuan on subsistence allowances, including 852 million yuan on subsistence allowance underwriting; from January to September 2018, the expenditure on rural subsistence allowances was 1.932 billion yuan, including a subsistence allowance underwriting expenditure of 745 million yuan, with a year-on-year increase of 19.76% and 16.6%, respectively. With the increase in the number of recipients, the pressure to raise funds for social assistance is also increasing.

According to above-mentioned research, the Central Committee of the TDSL pointed out in its "Proposal on Strengthening the Link between Social Assistance and Targeted Poverty Alleviation to Improve Its Effectiveness" that the relocation subsidy standard should be set objectively, and raised appropriately. It also suggested that a certain proportion of collective business construction land should be appropriately allocated in the relocation sites where conditions allow, urban residents should be permitted to purchase houses in the relocation sites or to cooperate with farmers to build houses, and the infrastructure and business facilities of the relocation sites should be improved.

...

All these proposals are based on the concerns and aspirations of the people. The year 2020 was when the goal of building a moderately prosperous society in all aspects achieved, and the year when the battle against poverty was won. To accomplish this goal, the CPPCC members, the political parties, and social organizations had always hold on to the original objectives, and, under the strong leadership of the Communist Party of China, worked hand in hand with the people to achieve the victory.

(**Contributed by Liu Tong, Reporter from Current Affairs Department,** *CPPCC Daily*)

No. 3743, the Third Session of the 12th CPPCC National Committee

The Proposal to Implement Brand Strategy to Promote the Transformation from "Made in China" to "Created in China"

6

PROFILE OF THE PROPOSER

The Committee on Economic Affairs of the CPPCC National Committee, one of the special committees set up by the CPPCC National Committee, is a working body under the leadership of the Standing Committee and the Chairmen Meeting of the CPPCC, and carries out in-depth investigation and research on the general policies of the country and on important issues in economic and social development according to the tasks proposed by the plenary and standing meetings of the CPPCC, and puts forward opinions and suggestions to the Central Committee of the CPC and the State Council through research reports, CPPCC information and speeches at the conferences.

The Birth of "China Brand Day"

With the intensification of economic globalization and international market competition, the world has entered the era of the brand economy. According to statistics, 20% of the dominant brands in developed countries occupy 80% of the global market share, and the international market has developed from price competition and quality competition to brand competition. Whether a country can benefit from globalization depends on whether it participates in, and in what way it joins, the global value chain system. Currently, a few developed countries have long occupied the middle and high-end positions in this global value chain, in which brand value plays an important role.

China has many products but less well-known brands as the world's second-largest economy. According to Interbrand's ranking of the 100 Most Valuable Brands of Global Enterprises in 2014, 54 were in the United States, seven in Japan, and three in South Korea. Huawei was the only Chinese brand on the list, ranking 94th, which is highly disproportionate to the size and international status of our economy, and reflects the gap between the quality of our economic development and that of developed countries.

The Shortage of Brand Development in China

In retrospect, two major setbacks have occurred in China's 30 years of brand development. The first time was in the 1980s when there was the selection of national, provincial and ministerial excellence brands—more than 6,000 were selected within ten years. Due to the lack of objective and impartial selection criteria, coupled with malpractice, the selection received strong criticism from society. The State ordered the selections to cease, because it was the positive energy of brands that market consumption needed. In 2001, the State approved the establishment of the world-famous brand and China's famous brand while banning more than 2,000 chaotic evaluation companies as well as the actions of spending money to buy brands. But only eight years later, in 2008, the Sanlu milk powder was found containing melamine that was fatal to babies, and thus, the State banned the selection of famous brands.

It is true that China's exposure of counterfeit and shoddy goods to protect the rights and interests of consumers on its annual "World Consumer Rights Day" is vital. Still, it lacks positive publicity and guidance for brands. Over time, consumers will only know what products are bad, but not what are good. For example, China has a number of dairy enterprises whose product quality has reached the advanced international standard, and most of the intelligent toilets in Japan are manufactured by Chinese enterprises. If they know about this, consumers will not mindlessly rush to buy foreign milk powder, let alone go to Japan to buy a toilet lid, and thus, they will become more confident in their own country's products. Chinese brands, consequently will also rise and have more demand at home and abroad.

It is common internationally to carry out brand value evaluation, and well-known global brand evaluation agencies usually refer to or adopt the evaluation rules, methods and standards of Western developed countries. There are three problems with such evaluations: firstly, the brand value evaluation lacks comparability from industry to industry and from sector to sector; secondly, the evaluation index lacks a scientific basis as it relies on only one financial indicator. And thirdly, it is subjective and unreasonable that countries with different systems adopt the same evaluation model. For example, in the U.S.-published "Top 100 World Brands" list, the U.S. has occupied more than half of the brands for many years, and Germany has long occupied about ten. China has few brands on the list, with Huawei as the only one with a relatively low ranking. China's Zhenhua Port Machinery holds 85% of the international market share but still does not meet the requirements of the evaluation. This reflects the importance of developing international standards for brand evaluation and controlling the discourse of international brand evaluation.

China's Access to International Discourse on Brand Evaluation

In 2012, China took the lead in proposing that brand value should include "quality" and "service" in addition to "tangible assets," and later the United States and Germany added two indicators of "intangible assets" and "technological innovation," respectively. After more than two years of in-depth exchanges, the "five elements" theory of brand value consisting of "quality, service, technological innovation, tangible assets and intangible assets" jointly proposed by China, the U.S. and Germany has been recognized and supported by many countries in the world. On this basis, in 2013, the joint proposal of China and the U.S. was voted on by 165 member countries of the International Organization for Standardization (ISO) for three months and 15 member countries of the Technical Committee for one month, and it had approval rates of 95.6% and 100%, respectively. In January 2014, the ISO Central Secretariat officially approved the establishment of the International Standardization Organization Technical Committee for Brand Evaluation (ISO/TC289)," with China as the permanent secretary country and the secretariat located in the China Council for Brand Development. China recommends the U.S. to be the first presiding country, with a five-year term. The presiding country will rotate among the members. Liu Pingjun, a 12th CPPCC National Committee member, was elected as the chairman of the advisory group. Austria, the U.K., the U.S., Italy, Russia, and 11 other countries are members, and 26 are observers. China has gained the international discourse of brand evaluation.

Proposal to Promote the Establishment of "China Brand Day"

On May 10, 2014, General Secretary Xi Jinping, during a tour to Henan Province, gave an important instruction, "promoting the transformation from 'made in China' to 'created in China,' from Chinese speed to Chinese quality, and from Chinese products to Chinese brand." He stressed that quality is the foundation, innovation is the soul, and brand is the goal. General Secretary

Xi Jinping's important instruction has clarified the direction for strengthening brand development and achieving high-quality economic development.

In the same year, the CPPCC National Committee member Liu Pingjun submitted a proposal on strengthening China's brand development, including establishing China Brand Day, etc. In 2015, the Committee on Economic Affairs of the CPPCC National Committee put forward a collective proposal on "Implementing Brand Strategy and Promoting the Transformation from 'Made in China' to 'Created in China'" based on member Liu Pingjun's proposal, which became a key proposal. It was later recognized as an excellent proposal by the CPPCC National Committee.

*Liu Pingjun, a member of the
CPPCC National Committee*

In January 2016, Yu Zhengsheng, chairman of the 12th CPPCC National Committee, presided over a fortnightly consultation forum on "accelerating the promotion of brand development," in which Liu Pingjun and 17 representatives of members, experts and entrepreneurs made key speeches. They proposed the establishment of China Brand Day, the establishment of the China Brand Research Institution, the establishment of a foundation for brand development, the reinforcement of protecting brand intellectual property rights, and other recommendations. After the meeting, the CPPCC National Committee submitted a special CPPCC information report, "Suggestions for Accelerating Brand Development," and Premier Li Keqiang gave important instructions in relation to this.

On April 24, 2017, to commemorate the day when General Secretary Xi Jinping made the remarks on "three transformations," the State Council approved to set May 10 of each year as "China Brand Day." The birth of China Brand Day aims to enhance the whole society's brand awareness, cultivate and promote the positive energy of Chinese brands, expand the market share of Chinese brands both at home and abroad.

Chinese Brand Development Achieved Important Results

First, a major breakthrough has been made in the international standards for brand evaluation.

As the secretary country of TC289, China organized the development of international standards for brand evaluation. After five years, the international standard of "Brand Evaluation—Principles and Fundamentals" (ISO 20671:2019) made by China was officially promulgated on March 12, 2019. China began to have a say in the international discourse on brand evaluation based on gaining international status.

Second, a brand evaluation mechanism with Chinese characteristics was initially established.

With the support of relevant state departments, the China Council for Brand Development has carried out six consecutive releases on the evaluation of public welfare brands, which the society has fully affirmed, and not a single letter of complaint has been received. At present, 25 national standards for brand evaluation have been promulgated, and ten other national standards have been formally established. China has gradually established a "scientific, fair, open and recognized" brand classification, evaluation, and release system.

Third, China's brand value has achieved a milestone.

British Brand Finance recently released the rankings of the world's top ten countries with the most valuable brands, and China leapfrogged to second place. During 2018–2019, China's brand value grew by 40.4%, to $19.5 trillion, the highest growth rate in the world.

Accelerating Chinese Brands' Entry into the World Market

Although China has achieved significant milestones, there is a long way to go for China's brand development. There is still much to do to speed up Chinese brands' entry into the world market.

First, to cultivate a brand cluster with international advantages.

American and European conglomerates often grow bigger and stronger through the acquisition and merger of dozens or even hundreds of enterprises, gradually forming a world-class multinational conglomerate. American conglomerates that have entered the world's top 100 brands usually experience 22 mergers on average, and possess an average of 200 well-known brands. For example, Coca-Cola has 275 famous brands, and Nestle has thousands of brands. In contrast, enterprises in developing countries are constrained by institutional factors, making it difficult to achieve strong alliances. The 19th National Congress of CPC pointed out that world-class advanced manufacturing clusters should be encouraged. After two years of research, it is better to promote about 50 internationally competitive industrial brand clusters to represent the image of Chinese brands and participate in the international competition of the brand economy. China wants to establish a global brand evaluation and release mechanism in accordance with the international standard of brand evaluation developed with China playing a leading role. It is also to establish a scientific and fair brand evaluation and publishing platform for the world, and to realize the joint development between group brands of developed countries and cluster brands of developing countries.

At present, China has established 32 brand clusters with international advantages, including tea, rice, self-cultivation, corrosion control, coking coal, bamboo and rattan, tea seed oil, consumer electronics, inspection and testing, power grid, Traditional Chinese Medicine, silk and mulberry, indoor air purification technology, etc. The brand clusters will represent the image of China in the world, and participate in the competition of the global brand economy.

China is promoting the establishment of the World Brand Federation, under which there would be an International Academy of Brand Science. In 2016, China, the U.S. and the U.K. signed a cooperation agreement to publish "World

Brand Evaluation Information" through the International Academy of Brand Science by the new international standard for brand evaluation (ISO 20671), to establish a more scientific and fair international brand value evaluation mechanism, and to promote joint development of the brand-based economy in countries with different systems.

Second, to develop regional brands and lead the high-quality development of the regional economy.

China has more than 2,800 products protected by geographical indication, more than the rest of the world combined. The international standard for evaluating geographical indication brands proposed by the Chinese delegation has been officially established. China has a long history and culture and rich resources, so it is essential to bring into play the advantages of China's regional brands with geographical indications, regional brands of tourist destinations, regional public brands of agriculture, and regional brands of cities, to achieve high-quality development of regional economy led by brands.

Third, vigorously promoting Chinese brands' positive energy through "China Brand Day."

Xinhua News Agency, Economic Daily, China Council for the Promotion of International Trade (CCPIT), China Appraisal Society and China Council for Brand Development jointly hold a China Brand Evaluation Press Conference and have the China Brand Day Gala every year on China Brand Day to boost the image of Chinese brands. We need not only World Consumer Rights Day to expose counterfeit and shoddy products to protect consumers' rights and interests, but also China Brand Day to promote outstanding brands and Chinese brands to the world.

(Contributed by Liu Pingjun, a member of the CPPCC National Committee, the board chairperson of China Council for Brand Development)

The Proposal on Accelerating Cooperation Between Guangdong, Hong Kong and Macao and Promoting the Development of the Pearl River Delta (PRD) Economic Circle

7

PROFILE OF THE PROPOSER

Yu Guochun, born in Indonesia in 1951, with his ancestral home in Meizhou, Guangdong Province, settled in Hong Kong with his parents in 1959. Currently, he is chairman of the Hong Kong Yuhua Group, chairman and general manager of Yuhua Domestic Department Store, chairman of the Hong Kong Guangdong Association, and permanent honorary president of the Hong Kong Jiaying Chamber of Commerce. He is a famous industrialist in Hong Kong and is known as the "king of domestic goods." In September 2018, he was elected vice chairman and standing member of the Tenth Committee of the All-China Federation of Returned Overseas Chinese (ACFROC). He was awarded honorary citizenship of Meizhou and the "Non-official Justice of the Peace" of the Hong Kong Special Administrative Region in 1992 and 1998 respectively. He was awarded the "Silver Bauhinia Star," the "Golden Bauhinia Star" and the Grand Bauhinia Medal in 1999, 2006 and 2019 respectively by the government of the Hong Kong Special Administrative Region.

Promoting Economic Development and Mutual Benefit in Guangdong, Hong Kong and Macao

---

Background

The Pearl River Delta (PRD) economic zone, a leading area of China's reform and opening up, is one of China's vital economic regions and manufacturing centers. Cities in this area serve as a hub for industrial investment from Hong Kong, and accelerate economic growth and complementary development by cross-border production, gradually gathering regional economic benefits and promoting the development of all kinds of industrial clusters with international competitiveness. In this way, the competitiveness of the core economic zone is continuously enhanced.

To further strengthen economic cooperation in the Greater Pearl River Delta (GPRD), the GPRD Business Council was established by the Hong Kong Special Administrative Region in 2004. Mr. Yu Guochun served as a member of the council from 2004 to 2010. The council, comprises members from different walks of life in Hong Kong (including the Chamber of Commerce, banking, shipping and textiles, accountancy, the law, logistics, technology, real estate, construction, environment, and education groups, as well as small and medium-sized enterprises and think tanks). The council hopes the members with rich professional knowledge and experience will exchange views on how to expand economic cooperation and exchanges between Hong Kong SAR and Guangdong Province.

The export of labor-intensive enterprises in the PRD was greatly reduced due to economic downturn, market shrinking and decreasing consumption caused by the international financial crisis in 2008. A large number of Hong Kong-invested enterprises in the region were also deeply affected, which made many Hong Kong business people anxious.

In 2009, for the first time, cooperation between Guangdong, Hong Kong and Macao was raised at the national level, as the State Council promulgated the "Outline of the Reform and Development Plan for the PRD Region (2008–2020)." Against the background of further economic globalization and regional economic integration, especially the spreading of the global financial crisis and its deteriorating influence on the real economy, the development of the PRD region was greatly affected. The negative impacts of the international financial crisis and remaining structural contradictions intertwined. So did the decreasing external demand and overcapacity in some industries. The same held true between drastic fluctuations in raw material prices and high dependence on the international market. In short, there were economic difficulties and deep-rooted contradictions and problems.

On the other hand, there were also major opportunities for the region: The shift of international industry to the Asia-Pacific region would not change. Regional economic cooperation and exchanges in Asia were on the rise. The process of the China-ASEAN (Association of Southeast Asian Nations) Free Trade Zone was being accelerated. China was still in a significant period of strategic opportunities in which economic development had a strong momentum because industrialization, informatization, urbanization, marketization and internationalization embraced further development and because economic integration in Guangdong, Hong Kong and Macao had been accelerated. In particular, thanks to the reform and opening up for decades, the PRD region had a strong material foundation, enhanced economic strength and regional competitiveness. All these had provided favorable conditions and a broad space for accelerating the reform and development of the region.

The Proposal

In April 2009, to grasp the opportunity given in the "Outline of the Reform and Development Plan for the PRD Region (2008–2020)" and put forward practical suggestions, the GPRD Business Council set up a special group, under the premise of win-win cooperation between Guangdong and Hong Kong. The Business Council also issued a report on key issues concerning industries and people's livelihood after half a year of the research, discussion and consultation. By doing so they hoped to promote the concrete implementation of the outline, boost cooperation in the area and explore new directions for economic reform and development in the future.

At that time, Mr. Yu Guochun was chairman of the Small and Medium-sized Enterprises Committee of the Hong Kong Special Administrative Region. In his continuous exchanges with people from all walks of life, he learned of the significant challenges and difficulties they had encountered during the financial crisis. Also, he learned of consensus about further cooperation between Guangdong, Hong Kong and Macao. Through in-depth research, Yu gradually realized that in the "post-financial crisis" period, it was a general trend to adjust the economic structure, upgrade the industrial sectors, vigorously develop the service industry, and accelerate the economic development of Guangdong, Hong Kong, and Macao.

In his opinion, the PRD region should seize the opportunity of the redivision of labor in the world economy at that time to strengthen cooperation with Hong Kong and Macao, to form a regional economic development model, and thereby build the GPRD Economic Circle into a world-class one comparable to New York and Tokyo. Driven by the regional economy, Guangdong, Hong Kong and Macao could complement each other by jointly developing producer services such as information processing and transmission, finance and insurance, and professional and technical services; on the other hand, they should focus on developing technology-intensive, highly interrelated, and strong motivating industries, such as new energy, new materials and new medicine. These efforts could build world-class industrial bases in terms of scale and quality and would also cultivate a number of world-class enterprises and brands with international competitiveness.

After careful preparation, during the two sessions (the annual NPC and CPPCC sessions) in 2010, Yu put forward the "Proposal on Accelerating Cooperation Between Guangdong, Hong Kong and Macao and Promoting the Development of the PRD Economic Circle." Facing existing problems in cooperation among these areas and difficulties faced by the business communities of Guangdong and Hong Kong in industrial upgrading and transformation and regional economic development, Yu presented in his proposal, five specific suggestions: (1) the government should reduce the limits of Hong Kong processing trade to domestic sales and treat all kinds of enterprises fairly; (2) the three local governments should jointly formulate a sound and internationally recognized testing and certification system, to improve the recognition and competitiveness of products in the international market; (3) the PRD region should strike a balance between labor supply and demand, to deal with "labor shortages" quickly; (4) local governments at all levels should make and implement specific policies and measures to protect the intellectual property rights of enterprises; (5) local governments at all levels should introduce a set of complete and sustained policies, to solve tax problems for enterprises which are undergoing transformation and upgrading. Among these suggestions, Yu particularly presented his expectation of the "one-hour living circle of Guangdong, Hong Kong and Macao," "183-day rule for personal income tax" and "border inspection between Guangdong and Hong Kong," as well as firm confidence in promoting cooperation between Guangdong, Hong Kong and Macao and in boosting the development of the service industry and economic upgrading and transformation.

Release of the "Outline Development Plan for the Guangdong-Hong Kong-Macao Greater Bay Area (GBA)"

Thanks to deepening cooperation between Hong Kong, Guangdong and Macao, economic strength and regional competitiveness in these regions have been strengthened substantially. The GBA has an excellent foundation for developing an international first-class bay area and world-class urban agglomeration. In addition, the deepening of the Belt and Road Initiative (BRI) makes it possible

The construction of the GBA being promoted

for the Bay Area to enhance its international competitiveness and participation in international cooperation and competition.

In 2019, the "Outline Development Plan for the Guangdong-Hong Kong-Macao Greater Bay Area" was formally promulgated. In this outline, there is a clear strategic positioning for the Bay Area: it will be built into a vibrant urban agglomeration, an internationally influential hub of science and technology and innovation, an essential pillar of the BRI, a demonstration area of in-depth cooperation between the mainland, Hong Kong and Macao, and a lively life circle suitable for living, working and traveling.

The outline sets goals in detail for the coming 3–15 years. First of all, by 2022, the comprehensive strength of the GBA would be significantly enhanced: cooperation between Guangdong, Hong Kong and Macao would be deepened and enlarged; driving forces in the area would be further enhanced; the framework would take shape for an international bay area with vibrant development, outstanding innovation capacity, optimized industrial structure, smooth flow of factors and a beautiful ecological environment. Simply put, a pattern featuring a reasonable division of labor, complementary functions, and diverse development in urban agglomerations would be established in the GBA. By 2035, the GBA will be home to an economic system and development model mainly supported by innovation, and a market of high connectivity. An international bay area suitable for living, working and traveling will be fully built.

One of the priorities of the outline is to establish and improve the development system of urban agglomeration, and to clarify the positioning and direction of central cities and important node cities. With Hong Kong, Macao, Guangzhou and Shenzhen as the core engines of regional development, we would continue to give full play to their comparative advantages and enhance their role in driving the development of surrounding regions. Zhuhai, Foshan, Huizhou, Dongguan, Zhongshan, Jiangmen and Zhaoqing should optimize the layout of the manufacturing industry. Zhuhai and Foshan on the west bank of the Pearl River should be home to the advanced equipment manufacturing industry cluster; Shenzhen and Dongguan on the east bank of the Pearl River should be home to the electronic information industry cluster with global influence and competitiveness. Dongguan should be supported to update its traditional sectors and Foshan should be a testing ground for the comprehensive reform and upgrade of the manufacturing industries. As for cooperation between the mainland and Hong Kong and Macao, three pairs of cities (Hong Kong-Shenzhen, Guangzhou-Foshan and Macao-Zhuhai) should establish alliances respectively, with Qianhai in Shenzhen, Nansha in Guangzhou and Hengqin in Zhuhai being three cooperation demonstration zones.

The outline not only sets regional and urban development goals on the macro level, but also pictures a convenient life model for 70 million people in the Bay Area in the future. The top priority is to build a "one-hour access" fast transportation network in the GBA. The outline plans on the intercity (railway) construction in the GBA, and accelerating the construction of the Shenzhen-Zhongshan Bridge and the Nansha Bridge. It plans to make new customs clearance models, give full play to the Guangzhou-Shenzhen-Hong Kong High-Speed Railway and the Hong Kong-Zhuhai-Macao Bridge, and promote the planning and construction of major new ports. In terms of trade, liberalization shall go on and the construction of a single window for international trade will be accelerated; in terms of finance, the outline plans to support the establishment of international commercial banks and financial institutions in the Guangdong Free Trade Zone, introduce high-quality educational and medical resources at home and abroad, and provide international high-quality social services. It also plans to support insurance institutions from the mainland, Hong Kong, and Macao in cross-border RMB reinsurance business and constantly improve the Shanghai-Hong Kong Stock Connect, the Shenzhen-Hong Kong Stock Connect, and the Bond Connect. In terms of the Internet, a comprehensive layout of the next generation of the Internet based on Internet Protocol version 6 (IPv6) will be carried out. The development of the wireless broadband city cluster in the PRD will be enhanced, and full coverage of free high-speed wireless LAN in key areas and key transportation lines in the GBA will be fulfilled. A high-definition interactive digital home network is on the way to achieve all urban fixed Internet broadband optical fiber access. In terms of education, cooperation in running schools by universities in Guangdong, Hong Kong and Macao will be strengthened. The outline plans to study how to enable primary and secondary school teachers and preschool teachers from Hong Kong and Macao to obtain teacher qualifications and teach students in Guangdong. It also plans to study how to give the children of Hong Kong and Macao residents working and living in the nine cities of the PRD the same right to receive compulsory education and senior high school education as mainland residents. In terms of tourism, international yacht tourism free ports will be constructed in appropriate areas. The outline also plans to explore and open tourist routes between Macao and neighboring cities and islands, and maritime tourist routes between Hong Kong, Shenzhen, Huizhou and Shanwei. In terms of medical care and elderly care, Hong Kong and Macao residents working and living in Guangdong will enjoy the same rights as mainland residents in education, medical care, pension, housing and transportation.

Building the GBA into world-class city clusters enriches the practical connotation of "one country, two systems." It will further strengthen exchanges and cooperation between the mainland, Hong Kong and Macao, and provide more development opportunities for Hong Kong and Macao and their residents. This way, China will maintain long-term prosperity and stability in Hong Kong and Macao. Constructing the GBA is conducive to the implementation of the new development philosophy. It also helps deepen supply-side structural reform, foster new growth drivers, and achieve innovation-driven development to support the continuous enhancement of the innovation power and competitiveness of China's economy. It is helpful in further deepening reform and expanding opening up, thus establishing a new system of an open economy in line with international standards and building a new platform for high-level participation in international economic cooperation. It is beneficial to promoting the construction of "Belt and Road." Through the regional two-way opening, the GBA will develop into an important support area for converging the Silk Road Economic Belt and the 21st Century Maritime Silk Road. The development of the GBA is a major development strategy in the reform and opening up in the New Era, a new attempt to form a new pattern of comprehensive opening up in the New Era, and a new practice to develop "one country, two systems." It is planned, deployed and promoted by President Xi Jinping. It will further deepen cooperation between Guangdong, Hong Kong and Macao, promote the coordinated economic development of the GBA, and further enhance the supporting and leading role of Guangdong, Hong Kong and Macao in national economic development and opening up.

> *"I am delighted that some suggestions mentioned in the proposal have been adopted and implemented. As a participant and promoter of the construction of the Great Bay Area, I am honored to witness the economic development and mutual benefit of Guangdong, Hong Kong and Macao over the years."*

Yu Guochun firmly believes that the GBA will further explore and tap its huge potential and become the most dynamic region in the world, promote the diversified development of industries, and provide a broader living and development space for residents of Guangdong, Hong Kong, and Macao.

The New Era has laid out a new mission. In the development of the GBA, committee members from Hong Kong and Macao will maintain closer communication with all sectors of society, and work hard to contribute to the steady and long-term development of "one country, two systems," and the integration of Hong Kong and Macao into the overall development of the country. In this way, they take the historic responsibility of national rejuvenation, and share the great glory of a prosperous and strong motherland.

(Contributed by ACFROC)

The Proposal on Rolling out Detailed Rules for Rapid Implementation of Preferential Policies for the Development of Hengqin

8

PROFILE OF THE PRINCIPAL PROPOSER

He Dingyi, a member of the 8th to 13th CPPCC National Committee, has long been engaged with business, women's issues, charity activities and various economic and social work. She is currently deputy director of the Liaison with Hong Kong, Macao, Taiwan and Overseas Chinese Committee of the 13th CPPCC National Committee, a member of the Standing Committee of the All-China Women's Federation (ACWF), president of the Macao Women's Federation, vice president of the Macao Chinese General Chamber of Commerce, vice president of the Industrial Association of Macao, vice chairwoman of the Supervisory Board of Macao Tong Sin Tong, and a member of the Advisory Committee for the Development of Hengqin New Area in Zhuhai.

In 1989, she became a member of the Standing Committee Advisory Committee for the Basic Law of Macao and the convenor of the Task Force on Economic Affairs. In 1998, she became the deputy secretary general of the Preparatory Committee for the Macao Special Administrative Region (MSAR).

In 2005, she was awarded the Order of Merit for Industry and Commerce by the MSAR Government; in 2012, she was awarded the Order of Merit of the Silver Lotus by the MSAR government.

Hengqin Development: An Active Exploration to Promote the New Practice of "One Country, Two Systems" with Macao Characteristics

Hengqin, a beautiful island with an area of 106.46 square kilometers, is more than three times the size of Macao, and is 187 meters away from Macao at its closest point. Macao and Hengqin are like two "zithers," one small and one big, lying across the vast South China Sea. As the wind blows, the rain hits, the tide strikes, the waves come, and the "zithers" sing harmoniously, pleasant to the ear.

The year 2019 is the 20th anniversary of Macao's return to the motherland and the 10th anniversary of the establishment of Hengqin New Area. General Secretary Xi Jinping had inspected Hengqin four times during the previous decade and paid particular attention to every step of Hengqin's development. He said, "At present, it is imperative to successfully develop Hengqin with the cooperation of Zhuhai and Macao to open up a wide space and inject new momentum for the long-term development of Macao."

Hengqin is a place full of opportunities and stories. It is not only an important platform to promote Macao's integration into the country's overall development, but also an active way of exploring the concept and practice of "one country, two systems." It has witnessed the unremitting efforts of the CPPCC members in Macao to perform their duties and responsibilities, to offer advice and suggestions in government affairs, and to build consensus. In 2019, on the occasion of the 70th anniversary of the founding of the CPPCC, the CPPCC National Committee honored the 100 most influential proposals from more than

140,000 proposals made over the past 70 years since the founding of the CPPCC. The proposal I made in 2012 together with member Lin Jincheng—"Proposal on Rolling out Detailed Rules for Rapid Implementation of Preferential Policies for the Development of Hengqin" was fortunate enough to be selected. While I am excited and honored, I look back on the past and remember it vividly.

Remembering the Original Intention: Enriching the New Practice of "One Country, Two Systems" and Creating a Better Tomorrow for Macao

At 00:00 on December 20, 1999, the five-star red flag and the flag of the MSAR were raised to the sound of the national anthem, and Macao returned to the embrace of the motherland. Under the policy of "one country, two systems" and with the strong support of the motherland, Macao has a new look: a rapid stabilization of law and order, and tremendous economic and social development. However, the small size of Macao, only about 30 square kilometers, limited land resources, and the fact of having gambling as the primary business have seriously constrained its development.

On January 10, 2009, Xi Jinping, then vice president of the PRC, visited Macao. At that time, when Macao was struggling to cope with the international financial crisis, Xi Jinping's visit brought not only good wishes, confidence and joy to Macao, but also a great gift: the announcement of the development of Hengqin Island. The development of Hengqin entered a new era, and all sectors in Macao rejoiced.

In August 2009, the State Council approved the "Overall Development Plan of Hengqin," granting Hengqin a preferential policy "more advantageous than the special economic zone." This is a product of China's reform and opening up, the fruit of scientific development thinking and the wisdom of contemporary human development of new areas. Hengqin was to be developed into a model zone for exploring new modes of cooperation among Guangdong, Hong Kong and Macao under "one country, two systems," a pioneer zone for deepening the reform and opening up and scientific and technological innovation, and a new platform for promoting industrial development on the west bank of the Pearl River.

On December 16, 2009, the Hengqin New Area was launched and on

December 20, the groundbreaking of the University of Macao's new campus on Hengqin Island took place in the presence of President Hu Jintao, who laid the foundation stone.

In March 2010, the Government Work Report at the NPC (National People's Congress) again actively emphasized promoting the development of Hengqin Island.

On November 14, 2010, Premier Wen Jiabao once again walked into Hengqin as a cheerleader for this new area of southern Guangdong.

On March 6, 2011, the Guangdong provincial government and the MSAR government signed the "Framework Agreement on Macao-Guangdong Cooperation" at the Great Hall of the People in Beijing, further decentralizing power from the central government to give strength to the development of Hengqin. As a major cooperation project between Guangdong, Hong Kong and Macao, the development of Zhuhai Hengqin New Area was written into the "Outline of the 12th Five-Year Plan for National Economy and Social Development of the People's Republic of China."

What is particularly memorable and moving is that on October 22, 2018, General Secretary Xi Jinping inspected Hengqin for the fourth time in ten years and pointed out that "the original intention of building Hengqin New Area is to create conditions for the diversified development of Macao's industries. Hengqin has the innate advantage of Guangdong-Macao cooperation, and it should strengthen policy support, enrich the content of cooperation, expand the space for cooperation, develop new industries, and promote more dynamic economic development in Macao." General Secretary Xi Jinping's speech pointed out the direction and provided fundamental guidelines for promoting a new round of development and opening up of Hengqin and promoting the diversified development of Macao's industries.

In February 2019, the "Outline Development Plan for the Guangdong-Hong Kong-Macao Greater Bay Area" was introduced, in which Hengqin development is mentioned in many places. In Section 3 of Chapter 10, it is specified that "promoting the demonstration of in-depth cooperation among Guangdong, Hong Kong, Macao and Hengqin in Zhuhai," which reflects the central government's attention to the cooperation between Macao and Hengqin, bringing new opportunities for the development of Macao. It strengthened the confidence of Macao compatriots to deepen the cooperation with Hengqin and integrate themselves into the country's overall development. With this new attitude, a new national area with long-established momentum and unlimited potential has finally come into the limelight.

Looking back on the ten years of Hengqin's development and construction, the past is as vivid as yesterday. Back in 2012, two years after the "Overall Development Plan of Hengqin" was introduced, and more than half a year after the State Council approved the policies related to the development of Hengqin, the implementation details of the preferential policies related to Hengqin development had not been announced. At this time, the Macao community responded enthusiastically to the central government's policy of supporting the development of Hengqin, and the industry was actively planning to invest and develop in Hengqin. Many people asked me for information and advice on the investment prospects, business environment, and preferential policies of Hengqin, including tax concessions, customs clearance system, innovative measures, industrial access policies, etc. However, because the specific implementation details had not been announced, I could not answer their questions, and people said that they could only wait and see. I felt that implementing a good national plan depends greatly on the details. Otherwise, "the door is open, but the communication channel is not open," and the policies still cannot be implemented. Only by better promoting the implementation of the "Overall Development Plan of Hengqin" can we better integrate Macao into the country's overall development, promote regional cooperation, and facilitate the diversified development of Macao's economy.

The motherland has always strongly backed Macao's development. As a member of the CPPCC National Committee, I always bear in mind the great responsibility and glorious mission I have to shoulder, always caring about the development of the country and the prosperity of Macao. I always try to help the practice of "one country, two systems" with Macao characteristics move forward steadily. I always hope for a better tomorrow for Macao and the motherland. In 2012, Mr. Lin Jincheng and I conducted research on the specific implementation details of deepening the cooperation between Hengqin and Macao, listened extensively to the opinions from various industries in Macao, and submitted the "Proposal on Rolling out Detailed Rules for Rapid Implementation of

Preferential Policies for the Development of Hengqin" during the Fifth Session of the 11th CPPCC National Committee and received great attention from the central government.

Taking up the Mission: Promoting Practical Cooperation and Writing a New Chapter of In-depth Cooperation between Hengqin and Macao

The potential is limitless as countless individuals come together for this cause! As the most important "backbone" of patriotism and love for Macao, members of the CPPCC National Committee of Macao represent Macao society from all walks of life. They should perform their duties and responsibilities well in promoting Macao's integration into the country's overall development and maintaining its long-term prosperity and stability. In the "Proposal on Rolling out Detailed Rules for Rapid Implementation of Preferential Policies for the Development of Hengqin," the four suggestions we made have been implemented one by one, providing positive help to promote practical cooperation between Hengqin and Macao. Their main aspects are as follows:

First, formulate and issue detailed rules to rapidly implement the preferential tax policies for Hengqin's development.

In March 2014, the Ministry of Finance and the State Administration of Taxation officially announced the "Hengqin New Area Enterprise Income Tax Preferential Scheme" and related preferential policies, which levied a reduced corporate income tax at a rate of 15% on enterprises located in Hengqin's encouraged industries. This policy positively impacted creating a business environment similar to that of Hong Kong and Macao and building a new platform to promote the moderate and diversified development of Macao's economy. Accordingly, the corporate income tax rate of Hengqin New Area would be close to that of Hong Kong and Macao, which has made easier the entry of more Hong Kong and Macao enterprises and investors into Hengqin, and promoted the cooperation and industrial integration of Hengqin with Hong Kong and Macao.

Second, rapidly formulate and roll out the comprehensive rules for implementing the customs system and measures for importing and exporting innovative goods to and from Hengqin.

On June 26, 2012, the General Administration of Customs held a press conference in Hengqin New Area, Zhuhai, Guangdong Province, announcing the introduction of "Suggestions of General Administration of Customs on Supporting the Opening and Development of Hengqin New Area." The General Administration of Customs introduced at the press conference that the Customs had put forward ten aspects with 24 measures to support the opening up and development of Hengqin New Area, including accelerating the construction of port facilities, innovating customs clearance system and measures, giving full play to the advantages of the location, implementing preferential tax policies, accelerating the construction of Guangdong-Macao Cooperation Industrial Park, promoting regional economic development, promoting the construction of customs IT systems, supporting the construction of major projects, cracking down on illegal smuggling activities, and increasing customs protection.

At the 14th Session of the Standing Committee of the 13th NPC on October 21, 2019, the State Council put forward for consideration a bill authorizing the MSAR to exercise jurisdiction over the Hengqin Port / Macao Port area and the relevant extended area. According to the motion, after the relocation of Macao's Lotus Port to Zhuhai Hengqin Port, the MSAR is to lease the right to use the Hengqin Port area and related extension areas, and is to implement the jurisdiction of the relevant areas in accordance with the laws of the MSAR. After the relocation of Lotus Port to Hengqin Port, the Hengqin Macao port area and related extended area are under the jurisdiction of the MSAR per the laws of the MSAR, adopting the customs clearance mode of "cooperative inspection and one-time clearance," and adopting for the first time the innovative, localized model of "one-time authorization and phased implementation."

Third, promptly formulate and issue the Hengqin industry access and preferential list.

On March 1, 2013, the "Industrial Development Guidance Scheme of Hengqin New Area" was announced, and many of the eight categories and 200 industrial entries are closely related to Macao, including tourism and leisure, trade and commerce, finance, culture and creativity, medicine and health, etc. Macao investors can get involved in many fields. After that, a number of implementation details of the preferential policies granted by the country to

Hengqin were successively introduced, and there were more precise guidelines for Macao enterprises entering Hengqin.

Fourth, promptly formulate and roll out the administrative measures for Macao's traffic access to Hengqin.

On December 20, 2016, coinciding with the 17th anniversary of Macao's return to the motherland, Macao's single-plate vehicle access to Hengqin in Zhuhai was officially launched. This policy facilitates Macao residents' investment and employment in Hengqin and promotes synergy and innovative development between Macao and Hengqin. The channel is jointly supervised by three inspection units, namely Customs, Border Inspection and Inspection and Quarantine, each with its duties but cooperating closely with each other.

With the high degree of attention and active support from the central government and relevant departments, and the joint efforts of the Guangdong provincial government, the MSAR government, the Zhuhai municipal government and all walks of life, the construction of Hengqin New Area is progressing rapidly, the cooperation between Guangdong and Macao is deepening, and the beautiful blueprint is gradually becoming a magnificent reality. In merely a decade, from a frontier island with banana forests, green fields, and a few farms, the Hengqin New Area has developed into a modern new city with rapid changes, with many tall buildings rising from the ground. Today, Hengqin has an excellent ecological environment, good infrastructure and diversified cultural life. Those achievements are remarkable.

However, development never ends, reform never stops, and cooperation continually deepens. Due to the differences in the procedures and systems between Macao and the mainland, which restrict the convenient circulation of the factors present in Macao and Hengqin, it is necessary to design from the top, remove the practical and administrative obstacles that limit the development of Hengqin and accelerate the rule and regulation alignment. In the continuous attention and in-depth research carried out by CPPCC members in Macao, we always put the deepening of cooperation between Hengqin and Macao in a critical position. It is an essential platform for grasping and promoting the diversified development of Macao industries. In 2019, CPPCC member He Runsheng and I submitted the proposal on "Promoting In-depth Cooperation between

Macao and Hengqin," which was listed as a key proposal by the CPPCC. From November 18 to 22 of that year, Ma Biao, vice chairman of the CPPCC National Committee, led a research group of the CPPCC's Committee for Liaison with Hong Kong, Macao, Taiwan and Overseas Chinese to conduct a research trip to Macao and Hengqin on the theme of "Promoting In-depth Cooperation between Macao and Hengqin." It is the first time since the founding of the CPPCC that cross-border key proposal supervision and research has been carried out, and this was an important initiative to lead CPPCC members and the community in Macao to study and implement the spirit of the series of important speeches of General Secretary Xi Jinping on accelerating the development of Hengqin New Area and promoting the cooperation between Guangdong and Macao. It was also an important embodiment of the CPPCC members' courage to take up the mission and fulfill their duties and responsibilities. By conducting in-depth research and listening to views from all sides, the research team put forward a series of suggestions, which were highly valued by the relevant departments and actively studied and promoted.

On November 22, 2019, He Dingyi spoke at a seminar on the supervision and research of key proposals to promote the in-depth cooperation between Macao and Hengqin

The Fourth Plenary Session of the 19th CPC Central Committee proposed to adhere to and improve the multi-party cooperation and political consultation system under the leadership of the CPC. To promote national reform and opening up and the cause of "one country, two systems" in the New Era, CPPCC members at all levels in Hong Kong and Macao are an indispensable and vital force, so they should continue to carry out their mission, perform their duties and take an active role. To promote the in-depth cooperation between Hengqin and Macao, we need to continue to work hard and will undoubtedly have great success.

Looking ahead: Joining the Overall Development of China and Embracing the Bright Future of Macao's "One Country, Two Systems" Practice

In a long view of history, 20 years is short, but it is enough for many changes to occur. From 1999 to 2019, the light shone brightly on the Haojiang River—20 years of Macao's prosperous and stable development, 20 years of the tremendous success of the practice of "one country, two systems" with Macao characteristics, and 20 years of writing a new chapter in Macao's history. At the conference celebrating the 20th anniversary of Macao's return to the motherland and the inauguration of the fifth government of the MSAR, President Xi Jinping delivered an important speech, highly praising the remarkable development achievements of Macao in the past 20 years since its return to the motherland and solemnly proclaiming to the world with great pride: "We firmly believe that the Chinese people, including compatriots in Hong Kong and Macao, have the wisdom and ability to make the practice of 'one country, two systems' develop even further, to improve the 'one country, two systems' system, and to govern the special administrative region better." With the support of the country, Macao is continuing to tap and release the huge institutional dividends of "one country, two systems," closely integrating its development with national rejuvenation, exemplifying the original intention and strong institutional vitality of "one country, two systems."

The development of Hengqin is a grand blueprint that has been planned and finalized by the CPC Central Committee and the State Council, under the leadership of the governments of Guangdong, Hong Kong and Macao. The development of Hengqin is also an important platform with innovative methods to promote the diversified development of Macao's industries. In the past ten years since the establishment of Hengqin New Area, it has significantly changed and has made remarkable economic and social development, moving from "kicking off and laying the foundations" to a new stage of "enriching content and gathering popularity." Hengqin has already shown its extraordinary beauty to the world, and we believe that with the efforts of all parties, this zither of the South China Sea will play the strongest sounds of the times!

At present, the Hengqin–Macao industrial synergy and cooperation are deepening, the institutional system to serve Macao's development is gradually being established, innovation and entrepreneurship by Macao youth are flourishing, and the integration of the life and society of the two places is deepening. In addition to the economic, tourism and youth aspects, there is more and more cooperation between the two places in terms of people's livelihoods. In addition to the Hengqin Community Service Center of the General Union of Macao Neighborhood Associations, which has been inaugurated, there is also the "Macao New Neighborhood" project, which integrates the functions of housing, elderly care, education and health services for the residents of Macao in the mainland for the first time. Both sides have set up a task force and land arrangements have been made, with over 180,000 square meters of land available for the project. This is a dynamic way of speeding up the construction of a Guangdong-Macao In-depth Cooperation Zone in Hengqin, which will vigorously promote the coordinated development of social services and governance between Zhuhai and Macao and is of great significance to enrich Zhuhai-Macao cooperation further and to strengthen cooperation between the two places, promotion of people-to-people contact and enhancement of the well-being of the people in both places.

At this new historical starting point, we should intensify and accelerate the pace of deepening the cooperation between Macao and Hengqin with a more open vision, innovative thinking, and efficient mechanism. We should transform Hengqin into an optimal place for Macao residents to live and do business. We should also make it a demonstration area for in-depth cooperation between Guangdong, Hong Kong and Macao to contribute further to the Guangdong-

Hong Kong-Macao Greater Bay Area and to the continued success of the reform and opening up. In the great cause of promoting the in-depth cooperation between Hengqin and Macao and enriching the innovative practice of "one country, two systems," we, members of the CPPCC of Macao, will not fail in our mission, and we will take an active and positive role, and perform our duties.

"The golden age is not behind us but in front of us." Entering the New Era, we are closer to the goal of the great rejuvenation of the Chinese nation, and we are more confident and capable of achieving this goal than at any other time in history. By standing tall and looking far ahead, thinking of danger in peace, being pragmatic and innovative, being firm and confident, and carrying out our mission, we will surely create a new horizon for the practice of "one country, two systems" in Macao. We will surely achieve a new victory on the journey of national rejuvenation and attain immortal historical glory together!

(Contributed by He Dingyi, a member of the CPPCC National Committee, deputy director of the Liaison with Hong Kong, Macao, Taiwan and Overseas Chinese Committee)

The Proposal for Taking Effective Measures to Actively Promote Universal Literacy

9

PROFILE OF THE PRINCIPAL PROPOSER

ZHOU JIANREN (1888–1984), also known as Songshou or Qiaofeng, was a native of Zhejiang Province and the younger brother of Lu Xun. He was one of the founders of the China Association for Promoting Democracy (CAPD), a famous modern social activist, a biologist, an expert on Lu Xun studies and one of the pioneers of the women's liberation movement. He was a member of the 1st and 2nd NPC Standing Committee, vice chairman of the 3rd to 5th NPC Standing Committee; a standing member of the 2nd and 3rd CPPCC National Committee; a member of the 1st and 2nd Central Council of CAPD, a standing member of the 3rd Central Council of CAPD; vice chairman and acting chairman of the 4th and 5th Central Committee of CAPD, and chairman of the 6th and 7th Central Committee of CAPD.

Universal Literacy Is a Basic National Policy that Has Been Given Top Priority

In September 1980, at the Third Session of the 5th CPPCC National Committee, Zhou Jianren submitted a proposal for "Taking Effective Measures to Actively Promote Universal Literacy for the Benefit of the Four Modernizations."

China's modernization entered a completely new phase after the Third Plenary Session of the 11th Central Committee of the CPC. The focus of China's work shifted to modernization, and the implementation of the Four Modernizations (modernization of agriculture, industry, national defense, and science and technology) began to be comprehensively promoted.

In implementing the Four Modernizations, the old generation of workers of CAPD showed great passion for their work. Zhou Jianren wrote in 1980: "The 4th Congress of the CAPD held in October last year clarified the nature and tasks of the Congress. After this congress, members worldwide generally felt a stronger sense of honor and responsibility . They would dedicate their lifetimes to the noble cause of the Four Modernizations." In the face of the passion of the members for the construction of the Four Modernizations, Zhou Jianren published an article "To produce 'three guidelines' for the Four Modernizations" in the *CAPD Newsletter* at the beginning of 1980, in which he proposed that the members of the association should "produce more results, more talents and more ideas" for the construction of the Four Modernizations. He called on members to give full play to their expertise, to accomplish the tasks entrusted to them by the Party and the people, to cultivate a large number of qualified talents for the country, and to express their opinions and make suggestions on the country's general policies and work in various aspects.

Even though Zhou Jianren was already 92 years old in 1980 and could not participate in field trips and research, he did not stop thinking about the construction of the Four Modernizations. Still, he used his expertise to study the Four Modernizations in China from the perspective of universal literacy. Zhou Jianren was a teacher when he was young. After the founding of the PRC, he served as the vice minister of the Ministry of Higher Education. He devoted himself to cultivating the ethos of diligent learning and a down-to-earth scientific attitude among university students. He dedicated his efforts to creating the first generation of intellectuals in New China. When he saw that the "Gang of Four" had ruined the young generation, and that there was a shortage of talents in the fields of culture, education, science, technology and health care, he felt despondent. He profoundly understood the importance of education and talents for the construction of the Four Modernizations. He realized that intellectuals form a valuable asset of the country and the backbone on the march

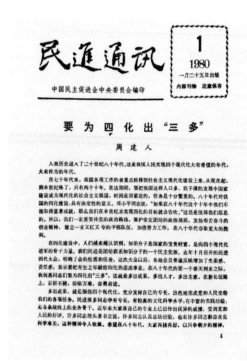

In the early 1980s, Zhou Jianren published an article in the CAPD Newsletter, calling on CAPD members to give full play to their own strengths and produce more results, talents and ideas for the "Four Modernizations," and at the CPPCC meeting in the same year, the CAPD submitted the proposal "Taking Effective Measures to Actively Promote Universal Literacy for the Benefit of the Four Modernizations."

to the Four Modernizations. The country needed a large number of competent personnels, especially primary and secondary school students of the 1980s, who would be the successors in constructing the Four Modernizations. In particular, he pointed out, "We should insist on giving equal importance to intellectual education, sports, science and technology on the education front." "Most of our comrades in CAPD are primary and secondary school teachers, who shoulder a great responsibility. We should not only teach students knowledge, but also teach them to be decent people. If we fail, the loss will be incalculable." As a result, at the 1980 CPPCC Congress, he submitted, as the principal proposer, the proposal of "Taking Effective Measures to Actively Promote Universal Literacy for the Benefit of the Construction of the Four Modernizations."

It was mentioned in the proposal that in the past thirty years, since the founding of the PRC, there had been achievements in education, and there had been some good experiences in popularizing education. However, on a national scale, the task of popularizing education was still far from being completed. The reasons for this included the lack of awareness of the importance and the lack of committed and effective measures for its development. After the smashing of the "Gang of Four," although the call for improving the scientific and cultural level of the entire Chinese nation was put forward, the popularization of literacy was still ineffective. Due to changes in rural distribution policies, there were school-age children dropped out of school in many places, which was worrying in the long run.

To build a modern, highly democratic and civilized socialist country, China must actively promote universal literacy. From the economic point of view, the construction of the Four Modernizations depended on high-level scientific and technological personnel, and there must also be a large number of educated and skilled laborers who could adapt to and master modern means of production. From the political point of view, the promotion of socialist democracy, the implementation of the Party's lines and policies, the implementation of the national legal system, and even the eradication of bureaucracy were all related to the education level of the people. Therefore, universal literacy must be achieved. From the social point of view, only when people were literate and well-educated could they truly establish a noble socialist moral style, eradicate feudal remnants, resist corrupt ideas, and strengthen social stability and unity.

The proposal held that universal literacy was a basic national policy and a primary plan for the country; for the people, it was like a "basic ration," not optional. The education cycle was very long, and we should take early measures to get it right. The proposal suggested that strong measures should be taken to promote universal literacy.

The proposal offered mainly seven measures to achieve universal literacy. First of all, the proposal called for strengthening publicity and education. It is essential to enhance the awareness of the whole society, firstly the cadres at all levels, of the importance of universal literacy, thus doing good work in the universalization of literacy for the future of the country and the nation. Second, in current conditions, the country should provide a deadline for universal primary education in rural areas, and universal junior high school education in urban areas. For those regions with difficulties, the People's Congress at the same level shall full discuss and submit an application to postpone. The suspension of universal education in those regions shall be only allowed with the approval of the higher level government. Attention should be paid to the census and education work in ethnic minority areas. Third, it should be stipulated that universal literacy is the responsibility of local governments at all levels. The local governments shall be responsible for funding universal literacy, and the central government shall allocate a portion of the funding. The local people's congresses have the right to decide how to implement universal education in their regions according to their particular situation—implementation would not be uniform everywhere. However, the quantity and quality of universal literacy would be an important part of the performance appraisal of governments at all levels. They must be reported to the People's Congress at the same level and the government at the higher level. The country should praise and financially reward regions that achieve universal literacy early or on schedule. Fourth, it should be stipulated that education is both a right and a due obligation of citizens. The country should enact an education law as soon as possible, clearly stipulating that anyone who has not received basic education shall not be a state cadre; there should be a difference in salary and treatment for the people with high and low levels of education. On the other hand, current public officials should take remedial training and reach a certain level by a specific date. Otherwise, they cannot continue to hold public office. Fifth, the administrative department of education should be responsible for implementing universal literacy in each region; the results should be inspected and accepted by the higher-level departments. Sixth, it is necessary to develop continuation education and social education to consolidate and improve the results of universal education. Seventh, the country should gradually increase education funding according to the financial situation, and clearly stipulate that the funds earmarked for universal literacy should not be embezzled or diverted to other purposes.

The CPPCC National Committee studied this proposal and referred it to the Ministry of Education for study. The proposal has contributed significantly to educational development in China, strengthening the concept of universal literacy and facilitating the healthy, lasting and in-depth development of education for all.

In addition to calling for attention to education and universal literacy through proposals at the CPPCC National Committee, Zhou Jianren also called for more attention to teachers' issues and spoke out to improve teachers' social status and living conditions. On January 22, 1981, an incident occurred in Wan County, Hebei Province, where elementary school teachers were beaten. Zhou Jianren proposed writing a letter to the China National Radio (CNR) in the name of the Central Committee of the CAPD, calling on relevant parties to seriously deal with the perpetrators and effectively protect the schools' environmental safety and teachers' personal rights. In the first half of 1983, another serious incident of beating and insulting a female teacher occurred in Chongqing. This incident showed that some parts of our country discriminated against and harmed teachers egregiously, and it was impossible to calm the situation without punishing those responsible. On May 13, Zhou Jianren and Ye Shengtao, two highly respected leaders of the CAPD, sent a joint letter to the General Office of the CPC Central Committee, strongly requesting that the perpetrators be punished according to the law. The Secretariat of the CPC Central Committee attached great importance to this and immediately called the CPC Sichuan Provincial Committee and Chongqing Municipal Committee. After investigation and verification, justice was finally done for the victim, the perpetrators were duly sanctioned, and the dignity of teachers was maintained.

On May 15, *Guangming Daily* published the full text of the letter from Zhou Jianren to the newspaper's editor-in-chief, exposing the above incident and calling on the whole society to respect the legitimate rights and interests of teachers and uphold the dignity of the Constitution.

On May 15, 1983, the front page of Guangming Daily *published the full text of the letter from Zhou Jianren to the editor-in-chief of the newspaper, calling on the whole society to respect the legitimate rights and interests of teachers and uphold the dignity of the Constitution*

Zhou Jianren held important leadership positions in China's educational administration and was the political party's major leader. He made many efforts to implement the Party's education policies, develop education, and improve teachers' political status and living conditions. He devoted himself to the cause of educating people in the PRC, winning the respect of the majority of educators and the affection of all the members of the CAPD.

(Contributed by the Central Committee of the CAPD)

The Proposal on Strengthening the Supply Side Structural Reform and Producing a Top-Level Design for Medical Reform

10

PROFILE OF THE PROPOSER

The CPPCC circles of medicine and health comprise members specializing in medicine and health care. The circles participating in the CPPCC are the specific divisions of the various parties, people's groups, ethnic groups, and people from all walks of life participating in the CPPCC organization, and the organizational form of the CPPCC meetings, reflecting the various components of the Patriotic United Front.

Make Suggestions for the Reform of China's Medical and Health System Through Brainstorming

At the Fourth Session of the 12th CPPCC National Committee in 2016, members of the medicine and health circles deliberated on a proposal. As far as I know, the number of proposals submitted in the name of circles is not large. This proposal was both born out of necessity and resulted from brainstorming and idea collision.

It was born out of necessity because the reform of China's medical and health system has been in full swing since 2009. Especially since the 18th National Congress of the CPC, the people-centered development concept has been deeply rooted in people's minds. General Secretary Xi Jinping's put forward increasingly benefiting all the people with the fruits of reform and more equitably has also led CPPCC members in medical and health circles to think about how health reform needs to evolve and in what form they should contribute to the reform.

Moreover, before the Fourth Session of the 12th CPPCC National Committee, public opinion made the circles of medicine and health focus on advancing the reform of the medical and health system. Shortly before the session, a video of a girl ranting against scalpers in Beijing circulated on the Internet, in which the girl condemned the scalpers for pushing a registration fee of 300 yuan up to 4,500 yuan. She snapped, "Ordinary people have to spend so much money and effort to make an appointment with the doctor. We can't get to see the doctor even though we come here very early in the morning."

Later, at the ministers' passage after the opening ceremony of the two sessions (the annual NPC and CPPCC sessions), Li Bin, then director of the National Health and Family Planning Commission of the PRC, said, "I want to thank that girl. This (bitter criticism on the scalper) forced the search for a solution to the long-standing problem (the activities of scalpers)." Moreover, instead of complaining about this problem, Director Li proposed a specific way to solve it. She pointed out that a combination of measures was needed. On the one hand, comprehensive checks must be carried out in conjunction with the police and other departments. Hospital scalpers had to be severely cracked down upon. Meanwhile, information sharing and the real-name system for hospital registration had to be accelerated. On the other hand, it was necessary to enforce reforms, accelerate the hierarchical diagnosis and treatment system, improve medical services, and promote the appointment system.

The members also felt the importance attached by the central government to the reform at the Fourth Session of the 12th CPPCC National Committee, which opened on March 3. When the first group discussion was held on March 4, Yu Zhengsheng, a member of the Standing Committee of the Political Bureau of the Central Committee of CPC and chairman of the CPPCC National Committee, participated in the joint group meeting of the medicine and health circles. After listening carefully to several members (including Huang Jiefu, Wu Mingjiang and I), Chairman Yu reviewed China's achievements in the medical and health system reform. He also provided directions and ideas for us to implement the instructions of the General Secretary since the 18th National Congress of the CPC and the suggestions of the Central Committee of the CPC on the Thirteenth "Five-year Plan."

The issue of medical and health system reform had become ever more critical. Throughout the session, it became the central focus of group discussions in the CPPCC circles of medicine and health.

I think this proposal was also the result of brainstorming from the circles of medicine and health. The circles had nearly 100 committee members, including scholars from large hospitals under the Ministry of Health, experts from remote areas, medical staff, and entrepreneurs from pharmaceutical manufacturers, technicians, and administrative leaders. Before the session convened, members of the medicine and health circles also conducted a series of investigations and research activities. For example, in 2015 and 2016 (before the commencement of the fourth session), many members visited public and private hospitals in Fujian, Anhui and other areas to listen to opinions from the grassroots. These investigations and research formed the basis for discussions at the session. Of course, each member understood the situation differently, had different perspectives, and brought forward different opinions. Since the reform affected every member of society, everyone cared about it. Some members not in the circles of medicine and health were also very concerned about the issue. During breaks between meals and meetings, even when walking in the courtyard after dinner, they discussed the reform together. The atmosphere of discussion gave many members of the medicine and health circles very good impression. I think it was great that everyone could speak freely, open up their hearts, share their views, and work together to reach a consensus. For example, some members believed that the price of medical and health services, including the above-mentioned registration fee, was a result of market behavior and should be liberalized. However, other members considered giving full play to market forces in this area was not helpful because healthcare was naturally scarce. The key was to distribute medical resources in a new way. The clash of ideas occurred every day in every group discussion and conference presentation.

In particular, at this session, the coordinated promotion of the linkage reform of medical care, medical insurance, and medicine was for the first time mentioned in the work report by the State Council. It gained tremendous interest among the members. Many members believed that it should constitute the guideline for reform. In the past, the linkage reform between three medical areas did not work. After piloting the reform of public hospitals for many years, no model could be replicated nationwide. Why? Members said that the reform was still incomplete, and the overall management of medical security and services had not been achieved; the problems in pharmaceutical distribution had not been eradicated; there existed a general shortage of high-quality resources for medical services, weak grassroots capacity, and restricted price flexibility. Due to the medical insurance compensation and the affordability for patients, the compensation system for medical staff was a complex problem to solve. Even though policies were issued, there were practical difficulties in funding them. When it came to issues in the health sector, members expressed their ideas vigorously and eagerly. Some members thought that the biggest obstacle at that time was the realization of "remote medical insurance."

I remember there were media reported that the topic of medical services was the most intensely-discussed topic in group discussion, and it was generally considered a challenging problem. Medical investment by the government was increasing year by year. Still, on the one hand, doctors felt that the medical fees were too low to reflect the value of their service, and patients complained about "inconvenient and expensive medical treatment" on the other hand. Some members felt that the current social focus on medical insurance integration was adjusting institutions and which department is responsible for each issue. But what should be more important was the scope, content and specific measures of medical insurance integration.

It was during these discussions that members reached a consensus step by step. Some proposed this consensus be presented in a proposal. The proposal should be submitted to relevant departments to promote reform. This proposal focused on structural suggestions, including the structural problems of medical services themselves (such as what to do with the people's hospitals at the county, provincial, and central levels), as well as how to solve problems about coordinated reforms in medical treatments, medical insurance and medicine in the government management system. This proposal was later rated as one of the 100 most influential proposals since the establishment of the CPPCC National Committee.

Participating in preparing and presenting this proposal also enabled me to understand the work better. A good proposal should list public concerns, focus on the central work of the CPC and the country, and suggest feasible solutions to problems. Thanks to this proposal, the CPPCC National Committee listed "deepening the reform of the medical and health system" as a critical issue in 2016 and held a seminar. Three research teams, each led by a vice chairperson of the CPPCC, conducted in-depth researches among the public. After their investigations, they proposed suggestions for medical reform and the medical insurance management system, the training of family doctors, the hierarchical diagnosis and treatment system, the medical insurance payment system reform, and the computerization of health information, etc. The proposal and its suggestions were adopted.

(Contributed by Fang Laiying, a member of the CPPCC and the Proposal Committee of the CPPCC)

The Proposal to the Bureau of the Legislative Affairs under the State Council to Research on the Enactment of the Law on the Protection of Children and Teenagers

11

PROFILE OF THE PRINCIPAL PROPOSER

KANG KEQING was born in September 1911 in Wan'an County, Jiangxi Province. She joined the Chinese Socialist Youth League in 1926, went to Jinggang Mountain in September 1928, joined the Red Army, and joined the CPC in 1931. In 1934, she was elected as an alternate member of the Executive Committee of the Provisional Central Government of the Chinese Soviet Republic. During the Long March, she served as the secretary of the General Branch of the Fourth Red Front Army Party School. After the founding of New China, she served as a member of the 1st, 2nd and 3rd sessions of the CPPCC National Committee, a member of the 4th standing committee of the CPPCC, vice-chairwoman of the 5th, 6th and 7th sessions of the CPPCC, a member of the standing committee, vice-chairwoman, chairwoman and honorary chairwoman of the All-China Women's Federation, secretary-general, vice-chairwoman and chairwoman of Chinese People's National Committee for Children's Defense, chairwoman of the Song Qingling Foundation and chairwoman of China Children and Teenagers' Fund. She was a delegate to the CPC's 7th to 13th National Congresses and a member of the CPC's 11th and 12th Central Committee.

A Solid Legal Shield for the Strong and Healthy Growth of Children and Teenagers

Children and teenagers are the flowers of the motherland and the hope of the nation. The answer to the question of how to let the flowers of the motherland bloom under the sun and how to provide a solid legal umbrella for the robust and healthy growth of children and teenagers starts with a proposal.

In April 1988, at the First Session of the 7th CPPCC National Committee, Kang Keqing submitted a proposal jointly with 21 members including He Zehui and Zhang Ziqing—"The Proposal to the Bureau of the Legislative Affairs under the State Council to Research on the Enactment of the Law on the Protection of Children and Teenagers." Children and teenagers are a special group whose physical and mental development has not yet matured and have unique physical and psychological characteristics. It was hoped that the Bureau of Legislative Affairs under the State Council would consider the issue of independent legislation for children and teenagers. Per their physical and mental development characteristics, the bureau should work with relevant units to formulate a child and teenager protection law as early as possible to protect their legitimate rights and interests.

As the first proposer, Kang Keqing pioneered in the case of protecting children's rights and interests and significantly contributed to the cause. In the autumn of 1944, the Central Committee of the CPC decided to prepare for the establishment of a nursery in Yan'an, and Kang Keqing was in charge of it. On June 1, 1945, the second nursery in Yan'an was officially opened for

In the mid-1980s, Kang Keqing was with children

children—this was the first nursery founded by the CPC. After the founding of New China, she actively mobilized all social forces to protect the rights and interests of children, set up nurseries in factories, rural areas, institutions, and communities, advocated and promoted the establishment of the National Coordinating Committee for Children and Teenagers Work and the China Children and Teenagers' Fund. Kang Keqing devoted herself to the cause of children with motherly affection, and people respectfully and affectionately called her "Mama Kang" and "Granny Kang."

The Bureau of Legislative Affairs under the State Council attached great importance to the proposal, and studied and handled it thoughtfully. In August 1988, it actively coordinated with the Central Committee of the Communist Youth League of China (CYLC), the State Education Commission, the Supreme People's Court, the Supreme People's Procuratorate and other departments to set up a national youth legislation leading group and its office, and jointly drafted the Law on the Protection of Children and Teenagers, so that the legislation for the protection of children and teenagers was put onto a "fast track" and entered a new stage in its development.

Ten Years to Sharpen a Sword

As early as August 1978, the Central Committee of the CYLC and the State Education Commission started to conceive the research and drafting work of legislation to protect children and teenagers. In March 1980, the Central Committee of the CYLC held a symposium on it and proposed enacting laws protecting children and teenagers. This symposium was the first important meeting in China to discuss special legislation for adolescents, and became the starting point of legislative work for adolescents in China. After the meeting, the Central Committee of the CYLC took the lead in researching and drafting the Law on the Protection of Children and Teenagers (Discussion Draft). Due to the lack of theoretical preparation and a strong public opinion environment, this draft did not, in the end, enter the legislative process in China. However, the symposium and the drafting of the law made a valuable attempt for special legislation for children and teenagers in China, which not only attracted nationwide attention, but also accumulated experience in practice for the study of legislation for children and teenagers in China and laid the foundation for the introduction of the law on the protection of minors in the future.

In October 1985, the Central Committee of the CPC issued the "Circular on Further Strengthening Youth Education and Preventing Juvenile Delinquency," proposing that "at present, the relevant laws for the protection of juveniles are not comprehensive enough, and suggesting that the legislature, in conjunction with the relevant departments, step up the enactment of relevant laws for the protection of juveniles in accordance with the spirit of the Constitution, and use legal means to protect the legitimate rights of juveniles from infringement." Youth protection legislation was placed in an important position.

In June 1987, the "Shanghai Youth Protection Regulations" took the lead. After introducing Shanghai's regulations, more than ten provinces and cities, including Beijing, Fujian, and Hunan, were enacting or preparing to enact similar local regulations. The practice of local legislation for juveniles has promoted the process of national legislation for juveniles. In August 1987, the Central Committee of the CYLC and the State Education Commission relaunched the research and drafting work on legislation for protecting minors.

In August 1988, the National Youth Legislation Leading Group integrated legislative resources. It formed a drafting group with experts from Peking University, China University of Political Science and Law and other universities. After much research and consultation, a draft law was formed after more than ten times of revision. The Bureau of Legislative Affairs under the State Council also did a lot of research and demonstration, and made four significant revisions to the draft. On September 4, 1991, the 21st meeting of the Standing Committee

中华人民共和国
未成年人保护法

PRC's Law on the Protection of Minors

of the 7th National People's Congress adopted the Law of the People's Republic of China on the Protection of Minors, which came into force on January 1, 1992. From the conception of legislative research to the introduction of the law, the name of the draft law was changed from the Law on the Protection of Juveniles to the Law on the Protection of Minors. The scope of protection was changed to apply to those under 18 years old, rather than to apply to those under 25 years old. The legislative intent covered not just the initial education to protect juveniles from corrupt ideas and the prevention of juvenile delinquency, but the comprehensive protection of minors. It is no exaggeration to describe this process as a decade of sharpening a sword.

The Introduction of the Law on the Protection of Minors

On June 28, 1999, the 10th Session of the Standing Committee of the 9th NPC adopted the Law of the People's Republic of China on the Prevention of Juvenile Delinquency, which came into effect on November 1, 1999.

The Law on the Protection of Minors and the Law on the Prevention of Juvenile Delinquency filled the gaps in China's justice for minors and together constituted the two pillars of China's legal system for minors, which plays an important role in creating a good atmosphere of care and love for minors in the whole society, effectively protecting the rights and interests of minors, promoting the all-round development of minors in terms of character, intelligence and physical fitness, and cultivating ideal, moral, educated and disciplined builders of, and successors to, the socialist cause.

The Laws Changing with the Times

With the deepening of the reform and opening up, rapid economic and social development, China's political, economic, social, cultural and other fields have undergone profound changes. Many new situations and problems have emerged in the field of juvenile protection, such as the increase of urban migrant children and the existence of a large number of left-behind children in rural areas. These children all require legal care; millions of children are addicted to the Internet and cannot extricate themselves, which requires a legal attention; juvenile delinquency presents a trend of younger age, which is a serious social problem and requires a legal response. At the same time, China has signed the "Convention on the Rights of the Child," the "World Declaration for the Survival, Protection and Development of Children" and other international legal documents. It is necessary to reflect these documents' elemental spirit and principles in domestic laws.

Members of the CPPCC National Committee had been continuously concerned about the healthy growth and legal protection of minors. Since the First Session of the 10th CPPCC National Committee, members had put forward proposals to amend the Law on the Protection of Minors at the CPPCC National Committee every year, calling on relevant state departments to amend and improve the law as soon as possible, further to clarify the rights and protection principles of minors, to clarify the responsibilities of the government and its relevant departments, to strengthen family, school, social and judicial protection, and to guarantee the effective implementation of the law.

At the same time, after more than ten years of law enforcement, many good experiences and practices in protecting minors had been accumulated in various places, and a series of relevant national and local regulations and policy documents had been issued. It was necessary to elevate effective and generally meaningful experiences and regulations into laws and promote them widely. Some laws relating to the Law on the Protection of Minors, such as the Criminal Law, the Criminal Procedure Law and the Marriage Law, had been amended one after another, and the Law on the Protection of Minors needed to be revised accordingly.

Following an active appeal by the CPPCC members and having to meet the requirements of the new situation, the revision of the Law on the Protection of Minors was included in the five-year legislative plan of the Standing Committee of the 10th NPC at the end of 2003, and the drafting work of the revision started. On December 29, 2006, the 25th Session of the Standing Committee of the 10th NPC considered and adopted the Law of the People's Republic of China on the Protection of Minors (Revised Draft), which came into effect on June 1, 2007. The revised Law on the Protection of Minors comprehensively reflected the latest developments in the protection of minors. It not only focused on the convergence with relevant international and domestic laws, but also addressed outstanding problems in reality, further expanded the scope of protection of minors' rights and interests, clarified the subject of law enforcement, strengthened and refined legal responsibilities, and enhanced the relevance and operability of the law.

On October 26, 2012, the 29th Session of the Standing Committee of the 11th NPC adopted the "Decision of the Standing Committee of the National People's Congress on Amending the Law of the People's Republic of China on the Protection of Minors" and the "Decision of the Standing Committee of the National People's Congress on Amending the Law of the People's Republic of China on the Prevention of Juvenile Delinquency." The amendments to these two laws brought together the efforts of the CPPCC National Committee members and fully reflected the CPC, the government, as well as the whole society's earnest care and love for minors.

To Build a Three-dimensional Protection Network

Since the 18th National Congress of the CPC, the Central Committee of the CPC, with General Secretary Xi Jinping at its core, has always taken healthy growth of children and teenagers as a fundamental national priority, cared for their healthy growth, and worked hard to create better conditions and environment for the growth of children and teenagers. It has pointed out the direction and providing fundamental guidelines for developing the cause of children and teenagers in the new era. The CPPCC members earnestly study and implement the spirit of the important speech of General Secretary Xi Jinping. In addition to making suggestions for the Law on the Protection of Minors and the Law on the Prevention of Juvenile Delinquency, which are being revised, they also contribute their wisdom and strength to constructing a comprehensive protection network for minors in various ways.

Minors are the "natives" of the Internet era. According to the "2018 National Study Report on Internet Usage by Minors," the number of underage Internet users in China reached 169 million, and the Internet penetration rate among minors reached 93.7%. While the Internet has brought convenience to minors' daily lives, it has also put them at a high risk for problems such as Internet addiction and cyberbullying. On September 21, 2017, the CPPCC National Committee held a biweekly consultation forum on the topic of "Creating a Clear and Clean Cyberspace." The members put forward their opinions and suggestions on strengthening the construction of network laws and regulations, improving positive energy online, and strengthening investment in and improvement of key technologies to create a clear and clean cyberspace for most Internet users, especially young users.

The Law on the Protection of Minors, which is under revision, has added the content of online protection for minors. However, the Law on the Protection of Minors can only provide overall regulations for the online protection of minors, and many systems for specific problems need refinement. From March 29 to April 4, 2018, the Committee for Social and Legal Affairs of the CPPCC National Committee and the Central Committee of the Taiwan Democratic Self-Government League formed a joint research group to conduct research in Shenzhen and Guizhou on the formulation of the "Regulation on Protecting Minors on the Internet." In the research, they went into enterprises, schools and communities, and met with government departments, legal experts, heads of social organizations, left-behind children and others for advice. On May 11, 2018, the CPPCC National Committee held a fortnightly consultation forum on the topic of "The Formulation of the 'Regulation on Protecting Minors on the Internet,'" where members, experts and enterprise representatives focused on the legislative orientation, general principles, basic system and regulatory system of the protection of minors on the Internet. They put forward their opinions and suggestions, forming consensus from all walks of life and vigorously promoting the realization of the regulation.

If the young people are smart, China will be intelligent; if the young people are strong, China will be strong. Today's children and teenagers are growing up in the reform era when the motherland is stronger and more prosperous, and in the great era when the Chinese nation is getting closer to achieving rejuvenation. With the loving care of the Central Committee of the CPC, with General Secretary Xi Jinping at the core, and under the protection of ever-improving laws, they will surely grow up healthily and be ready to realize the Chinese dream of the great rejuvenation of the Chinese nation!

(Contributed by Office of the Committee for Social and Legal Affairs of the CPPCC National Committee)

No. 0663, the Third Session of the 6th CPPCC National Committee

The Proposal that China Should Join the Convention on the Protection of World Cultural and Natural Heritage as Soon as Possible to Facilitate the Preservation and Protection of China's Major Cultural and Natural Heritage and Strengthen China's Position in International Cultural Cooperation

12

PROFILE OF THE PRINCIPAL PROPOSER

HOU RENZHI (1911–2013), born in Zaoqiang County, Hebei Province, was a famous Chinese historical geographer and academician of the Chinese Academy of Sciences. He graduated from Yanjing University in 1936 and received his PhD from the University of Liverpool, UK, in 1949. He opened up new ways and fields in the theoretical discussion and research on historical geography, urban historical geography and desert historical geography. He also provided fundamental knowledge of desert control and urban planning and construction. He systematically studied the origin and development of Beijing, the development of water sources in previous dynasties, and the characteristics of urban planning. He was a member of the 3rd to 7th CPPCC National Committes.

A Proposal that Helps to Kick off China's Application for World Heritage

————

As of July 2019, China has 55 world heritage sites (37 cultural, 14 natural, and four mixed properties), ranking as the country with the most world heritage sites with Italy. China's world heritage protection started in the mid-1980s and has continued for about 35 years till 2019. Over the years, this cause has taken root in China, developed rapidly, and made outstanding contributions to the progress of human civilization.

In retrospect, we cannot forget that China's world heritage protection started with a joint proposal made by four members of the CPPCC National Committee.

Part One

The initiator of the proposal is Hou Renzhi, an member of the Chinese Academy of Sciences, a famous historical geographer and a 3rd to 7th CPPCC National Committee member. At the beginning of 1984, Mr. Hou was invited to lecture at Cornell University in the United States. Previously, he did not know that the United Nations Educational, Scientific and Cultural Organization (UNESCO) had a "Convention Concerning the Protection of the World Cultural and Natural Heritage." In July, the *Beijing Evening News,* jointly with relevant parties, launched a social fund-raising activity for "Love China and Restore the Great Wall." The activities were carried out extensively and attracted international attention. Mr. Hou recalled that on July 26, he was invited to visit Professor McGrath working at the Department of Architecture at George Washington University. As soon as they met, Professor McGrath said excitedly that he had read the news about China's fund-raising for the restoration of the Great Wall in the *New York Times*. They talked about the maintenance and protection of ancient Chinese buildings and sites the whole morning. Mr. Hou said that they always spoke about these issues when communicating with American scholars. On one occasion, Professor Steinberg of the Department of Geography at the University of California, Berkeley, told him bluntly, "The Great Wall of China is such a wonder in the history of world culture. It belongs not only to the Chinese people, but also to the people of the world." They briefed Mr. Hou on the "Convention Concerning the Protection of the World Cultural and Natural Heritage," and hoped that China would join the Convention as soon as possible and contribute more to human culture and science.

On November 16, 1972, the 17th Session of the General Conference of UNESCO adopted the "Convention Concerning the Protection of the World Cultural and Natural Heritage" in Paris, which decided to protect and manage internationally recognized cultural relics and natural landscapes with outstanding and universal values as the common property of all humanity. To this end, it is to "establish a permanent and effective system based on modern scientific methods." In November 1976, the first general assembly of member countries of the "Convention Concerning the Protection of the World Cultural and Natural Heritage" was held in Nairobi, Kenya. The World Heritage Committee was officially established and the "World Heritage List" was established simultaneously. In 1978, the 2nd Session of the World Heritage Committee announced the first batch of world heritage sites (12 sites in total).

During his stay in the United States, Hou Renzhi wrote twice to Zhang Wei, a member of the Permanent Mission of China to UNESCO, asking whether China had ratified the UNESCO World Heritage Committee, whether it had proposed maintenance and protection projects, and whether it was ready to join the Convention. The reply was that these issues were under consideration and had not been finally decided, which gave Mr. Hou some anxiety.

Part Two

After returning home, Hou Renzhi always wanted to make an effort in this matter. In March 1985, when the Third Session of the 6th CPPCC National Committee convened, as a member of the CPPCC National Committee, Mr. Hou thought of making a joint proposal. He hoped the CPPCC National Committee would play a vital role in promoting this matter. In the proposal, he first introduced the "Convention Concerning the Protection of the World Cultural and Natural Heritage" and then wrote:

> *... China has ancient civilization, vast territory and abundant resources. The above-mentioned cultural and natural heritages are of great world value and should be actively preserved and protected. Countless heritages are recognized worldwide and have been actively sponsored by international friends for maintenance and protection. For example, the Great Wall and Wolong Panda Nature Reserve belong respectively to cultural and natural heritage. However, as China has not yet participated in the Convention, they cannot enjoy all the rights and interests that the signatory countries enjoy, and this is not conducive to promoting international cultural cooperation which is beneficial to all humanity.*
>
> *It is reported that China's National Commission for UNESCO has made a lot of preparations to participate in the "Convention Concerning the Protection of the World Cultural and Natural Heritage." The Ministry of Culture, the Chinese Academy of Sciences, the Chinese National Committee for Man and Biosphere Programme, the Ministry of Urban and Rural Construction and Environmental Protection, the Ministry of Forestry and other parties have also investigated this issue, but have not yet made a final decision together. At present, China implements an open-up policy. In addition to paying attention to the introduction of various technologies, equipment and funds conducive to the construction of material civilization in China's Four Modernizations, we should also actively participate in and promote international cultural and scientific undertakings beneficial*

to China and the spiritual civilization of the world's people. Therefore, I suggest China participate in the "Convention Concerning the Protection of the World Cultural and Natural Heritage" as soon as possible and prepare to join the World Heritage Committee.

It should be noted that, as an example, Hou Renzhi considered that the habitat of giant pandas should be declared a world natural heritage in his proposal. More than 20 years later, this project was successfully listed in World Heritage in July 2006 (according to the contributor).

Part Three

The second person who signed the proposal is Mr. Yang Hanxi, a famous ecologist and a member of the 5th to 8th CPPCC National Committees. Why was Mr. Yang invited? Mr. Hou explained that World Heritage includes not only historical and cultural sites, but also natural science and ecological environments. Mr. Yang was then secretary general of the Chinese National Committee for Man and Biosphere Programme.

According to Mr. Yang Hanxi, as early as 1982, he participated in the discussion on whether China should accede to the "Convention Concerning the Protection of the World Cultural and Natural Heritage." At that time, a foreign expert in the Chinese National Committee for Man and the Biosphere Programme first proposed that China should participate. It was confirmed by archives from China's National Commission for UNESCO. On March 19, 1982, The Permanent Mission of China to UNESCO wrote to the Chinese Academy of Sciences on the letterhead of "On 'Convention Concerning the Protection of the World Cultural and Natural Heritage,'" in which it was said:

Relevant members of our delegation recently met with Von Droste, an official from the Department of Ecology of UNESCO who was in charge of the "Convention Concerning the Protection of the World Cultural and Natural Heritage," and talked about the issue that the Department had sent a letter to Yang Hanxi, inviting China to join the Convention. He said that China was a country with an ancient civilization and rich cultural and natural heritage, and hoped that China would accede to the Convention as soon as possible.

Moreover, a consultation on the "Convention Concerning the Protection of the World Cultural and Natural Heritage" was held on August 28, 1982. Yang Hanxi was on the attendance list.

Part Four

The CPPCC session of that year opened on March 25. According to Mr. Luo Zhewen, Mr. Hou Renzhi met with him and Mr. Zheng Xiaoxie at the beginning of the meeting. He talked about the matter of putting forward a joint proposal with relevant members to promote China's accession to the "Convention Concerning the Protection of the World Cultural and Natural Heritage." Zheng and Luo could not agree more. Since they were going to Japan to attend an international conference on March 27, they asked Mr. Hou to draft and sign the proposal on their behalf. On the closing day of the CPPCC session on April 8, Mr. Hou did not see Zheng Xiaoxie and Luo Zhewen who had returned home. He wrote to Mr. Zheng Xiaoxie:

Midnight, April 9

Comrade Xiaoxie,

I am glad to hear that you and Zhewen have returned fruitfully from Nara. At the closing meeting of the CPPCC yesterday afternoon, I saw Mr. Shan (Mr. Shan Shiyuan, according to the contributor). I asked him if he had seen you and Zhewen, and he said he had met you in the hall. So I walked around the hall a few times, even stood on the stone steps in front of the Great Hall after meeting, hoping to see you. It's a pity that I didn't see you and Zhewen.

I received your letter you sent to Jingfeng Hotel the other day. I fully understand your concern about protecting cultural relics and scenic spots. It is your concern that drove me to draft the proposal. The full text of the "reasons" will be copied and sent to you. Now I copy the "causes" and "methods" parts as follows (omitted).

Yang Hanxi (National Committee for Man and Biosphere Programme) and I have signed. Besides, I have signed it on your and Zhewen's behalf. I believe he would agree, too. I didn't ask for more signatures, but I asked Yang Bozhen of the National Committee of China's Scientific, Educational and Cultural Organization for his opinions in advance, and asked him to read the full text. He also added some content.

There would be a lot of matters to deal with after returning to Peking University, so that I will tell you about this matter first. Please tell Zhewen about it as soon as possible (I don't have your and his phone numbers).

Best wishes!

Yours,

Hou Renzhi

Or, you can transfer this letter to Zhewen.

As mentioned in the letter, Mr. Zheng Xiaoxie and Mr. Luo Zhewen devoted themselves to protecting cultural heritage. Together with Mr. Shan Shiyuan, they were known as the "troika" in cultural relics protection.

Zheng Xiaoxie was a planning expert at the Ministry of Urban and Rural Construction and Environmental Protection at that time. Since he served as a member of the 5th CPPCC National Committee in 1978, he had devoted himself to protecting cultural relics, famous historical and cultural cities and world heritage sites. In February 1979, when he heard that the Arrow Tower, part of Deshengmen in Beijing, was to be demolished, he immediately wrote to Vice Chairman Chen Yun, calling for this to stop.

Later, Zheng Xiaoxie also contributed to the declaration of World Heritage of Pingyao Ancient City. In the pre-selection list discussed by relevant departments, Pingyao was not included. On June 19, 1995, four days after the seminar, he wrote to the Ministry of Construction and the National Cultural Heritage Administration leaders to explain in detail the reasons for adding Pingyao. Pingyao and Lijiang were declared world cultural heritage thanks to his efforts.

Part Five

Among the four members, Luo Zhewen was the "youngest" and was a member of the 6th to 8th CPPCC National Committees. In 1940, at the age of 16, Luo Zhewen was admitted to the Society for Research in Chinese Architecture in Lizhuang, Sichuan, and supervised by Liang Sicheng. From then on, he began his career in protecting and researching of ancient buildings.

Mr. Luo recalled that he and Hu Sha from the UNESCO National Committee had mentioned China's accession to the "Convention Concerning the Protection of the World Cultural and Natural Heritage" as early as 1979 when they received the director general of UNESCO. However, China's participation had not been started because the coordination among various departments was insufficient and there was much other work at that time. The Cultural Relics Bureau organized Hou Renzhi and other famous scholars to compile a book promoting Chinese civilization, which was not published for some reason.

Among the four proposers, Mr. Luo Zhewen was the only one who participated in the first application which began in 1986. As an ancient architecture expert of the State Administration of Cultural Relics, he participated in the declaration of China's World Heritage many times since then. In his life, Mr. Luo Zhewen devoted most of his life to the protection and research of the Great Wall, and advocated the application of the Beijing–Hangzhou Grand Canal for World Heritage in his later years.

Part Six

The joint proposal No. 0663 was submitted and soon attracted the attention of relevant parties. On November 22 of that year, the 13th Session of the Standing Committee of the 6th NPC decided to ratify China's accession to the "Convention Concerning the Protection of the World Cultural and Natural Heritage." On December 16, Cai Jintao, first Secretary of the Permanent Mission of China to UNESCO, and Amadou Mahtar M'Bow, then director general of UNESCO, signed the text of China's accession to the Convention at UNESCO headquarters in Paris.

In December 2005, at the symposium commemorating "20 Years of World Heritage Conservation in China," Zhou Tienong (fourth from left), then vice chairman of the CPPCC, presented bronze plates with the CPPCC emblem to four veteran members who had jointly proposed the event: Yang Hanxi (first from left), Zheng Xiaoxi (third from left), Luo Zhewen (fifth from the left), and Mr. Hou Renzhi was represented by his eldest son Hou Fangxing (second from right).

In 1987, six sites, including the Great Wall, the Forbidden City, the Mogao Grottoes in Dunhuang, the Mausoleum of the Emperor Qin Shi Huang and the Pit of the Terracotta Warriors, the Peking Man Site at Zhoukoudian, and Mount Tai were included in the "World Heritage List" by the World Heritage Committee. The curtain of China's World Heritage declaration has been unveiled since then!

"You burned your life for the cause of your motherland and left me here mourning you with tears." To borrow Mr. Zheng Xiaoxie's poem in memory of Mr. Shan Shiyuan, we deeply cherish the memory of the four senior members who have contributed significantly to China's world heritage protection.

(Contributed by Wang Wenyun, director of the First Editorial Office of the China Literature and History Publishing House)

No. 1412, the First Session of the 10th CPPCC National Committee

The Proposal for the Construction of the Conservation and Utilization Facilities of the Dunhuang Mogao Caves

13

PROFILE OF THE PRINCIPAL PROPOSER

FAN JINSHI, a CPC member and a native of Hangzhou, Zhejiang Province, was born in Beiping (Beijing) in July 1938. She is the former president, the current honorary president and research curator of Dunhuang Academy, a part-time professor and doctoral supervisor in Dunhuang studies at Lanzhou University. She was a member of the 8th to 12th CPPCC National Committee.

Digital Display of the Millennium Mogao, a Win-Win Outcome for Conservation and Utilization of Cultural Heritage

The Dunhuang Mogao Caves are a world-renowned cultural heritage site, a treasure of human civilization, and an example of Chinese traditional culture. Every year, millions of visitors from around the world visit the caves. Today, visitors to the Mogao Caves can experience scientific, standardized and people-centered cultural tourism through a "general control, online reservation, digital display, and on-site viewing" model. Visitors can enjoy a high-quality cultural experience through an immersive digital display of Dunhuang and its art, as well as an on-site visit to the Mogao Caves.

The Mogao Caves' practice of combining heritage conservation with tourism development has become a model of its kind at home and in the world of cultural heritage sites. At the 34th Session of the World Heritage Committee in Brazil in 2010, the experience of the Mogao Caves in Dunhuang was shared as a typical case study to the world heritage sites in various countries, with the General Assembly commenting, "The Mogao Caves have demonstrated with extraordinary foresight the effective approach to tourism management of heritage sites to protect their value, setting a significant example in this area."

The fruitful results started in 2003 when Fan Jinshi, then director of the Dunhuang Academy, submitted Proposal No. 1412, "Construction of a Visitor Center for the Dunhuang Mogao Caves," to the First Session of the 10th CPPCC National Committee.

Proposal Rationale: How to Resolve the Contradiction Between Conservation and Utilization of the Mogao Caves

The Dunhuang Mogao Caves, excavated between the 4th and 14th centuries AD, are the largest, most extensive, most prosperous, and best-preserved Buddhist cave complex worldwide.

More than 84% of the Mogao Caves are less than 25 square meters in size, and some are only a few square meters. The exquisite sculptures and murals are made of fragile materials such as clay, wheat grass, wood and pigments. Over the centuries, some caves have collapsed and been damaged by natural and human factors. The cave murals and sculptures have suffered from various degrees of hollowing, peeling, flaking, and nail damage and have gradually undergone a metamorphosis over time. Over the years, the Dunhuang Academy has always made the protection of Mogao Caves a priority.

Since the Mogao Caves opened in 1979, more visitors than ever have come to Dunhuang to enjoy the beauty of the art in the caves. There is an unstoppable growth in the number of visitors, but the trend is not without risk. Visitors entering the caves of Mogao can see thousands of years of precious and fragile painted sculptures and murals, equivalent to entering a museum's "relics vault" of fine art. Visits to the caves pose a significant risk to the cultural relics due to the potential danger of their destruction and the deterioration of their microenvironment. The continuing rise in the number of visitors has led to a growing conflict between the opening up of the Mogao Caves for tourism on the one hand and conservation management on the other.

In 2002, the Dunhuang Academy carried out the "Study on Mogao Caves Potential Visitor Capacity" along with the Getty Conservation Institute. It concluded that the caves open to the public cannot be less than 13 square meters, there should be no more than 25 visitors per group, and there should be a maximum daily visitor carrying capacity of 3,000 for the Mogao Caves. Under these premises, the parameters of the cave micro-environment will not exceed critical value and can protect cave artifacts while ensuring a good visitor experience.

As a specialized institution for the protection, study and promotion of the Dunhuang Mogao Caves, the Dunhuang Academy must neither sacrifice cultural artifacts to keep the Mogao Caves open for uncontrolled numbers of visitors, nor overdo the protection of the site to the extent of closing the doors of the Mogao Caves to visitors.

Questions like these preoccupied Fan Jinshi, then president of the Dunhuang Academy, and she worked hard to come up with solutions.

President Fan was inspired by the Dunhuang Academy's years of "Digital Dunhuang" practice. When Fan first encountered computers in the 1980s, she realized that computer technology could be used to create digital archives of Mogao Caves' relics for their "permanent preservation and sustainable use." In the 1990s, the Dunhuang Academy came up with the idea of "Digital Dunhuang" and collaborated with the Andrew W. Mellon Foundation and Northwestern University to use advanced digital cameras to capture the murals and sculptures of the Mogao Caves and create digital images. The virtual reality technology would render the cave murals more realistic and give the public an immersive experience.

Seeing the prospect of "Digital Dunhuang," Fan Jinshi couldn't help thinking: Can we try to use digital technology to get Mogao Caves' relics out of the caves, and then visitors can see them outside the caves, so that we can ensure the safety of the relics and bring the audience a high-quality, enjoyable cultural experience. After much deliberation, Fan Jinshi decided to submit her long-standing ideas on the conservation and utilization of the Dunhuang Mogao Caves to the CPPCC National Committee as a proposal.

Prudent Proposal: Construction of a Visitor Center for the Dunhuang Mogao Caves

At the First Session of the 10th CPPCC National Committee in March 2003, Fan Jinshi joined 24 CPPCC members in proposing the "Construction of a Visitor Center for the Dunhuang Mogao Caves." The proposal suggested that in the context of the rapid growth in the number of visitors to the Mogao Caves, an effective way to better protect this world cultural heritage site would be to build an infrastructure with digital conservation and utilization functions. Digital display technology would be used to bring the relics in caves outside for visitors.

The proposal was approved by the leadership of the CPPCC National Committee, and was listed as a key proposal by the Committee on Proposals. In August 2003, a joint inspection team of the Proposal Handling Committee of the CPPCC National Committee went to the Mogao Caves for a field study and research, and submitted a "Research Report on the Construction of Conservation and Utilization Facilities for the Dunhuang Mogao Caves" to the CPPCC National Committee. The report concluded that the idea of a project to protect and utilize the Mogao Caves in the context of China's national conditions, drawing on foreign advanced experience in the construction of conservation and utilization facilities, was not only an effective measure to fundamentally address the conservation and development of the Dunhuang Mogao Caves, but also would serve as a pioneering model in solving similar problems nationwide. The committee actively supported it and its urgent implementation.

The proposal also attracted the attention of the central leadership. Premier Wen Jiabao and State Councilor Chen Zhili gave important instructions in relation to the research report of the CPPCC National Committee: the conservation of Mogao Caves should be given attention and practical and feasible programs should be put forward.

In November 2003, the Dunhuang Academy commissioned the China Academy of Architectural Design and Research to complete a "Proposal for the Construction of a Conservation and Utilization Facility for the Dunhuang Mogao Caves" (hereafter Project Proposal). The Project Proposal was based on the current situation and demand for the protection and utilization of the Mogao Caves. It comprehensively assessed the need, urgency and feasibility of the construction. In February 2004, the Project Proposal was officially submitted to the National Development and Reform Commission. The project was formally approved on December 4, 2007, after organizing essential technical research with the participation of domestic and foreign heritage experts, and evaluation by the National Development and Reform Commission and the National Investment Project Evaluation Center.

In December 2008, the Mogao Caves Conservation and Utilization Project was initiated, consisting of four sub-projects: sand control, cliff reinforcement and palisade renovation, construction of security facilities, and construction of the Visitor Center (later renamed the Mogao Caves Digital Exhibition Center). The Mogao Caves Digital Exhibition Center was the core project, and Fan Jinshi was its project general manager.

Proposal Implementation: The Difficult Exploration of the Construction and Management of the Mogao Caves Digital Exhibition Center

The use of digital technology to showcase cultural heritage was utterly unprecedented at the time, and Dunhuang Academy was the "first to take the plunge." It was also a massive challenge for the Dunhuang Academy, which had no experience in large-scale construction, to undertake such an unprecedented and complex project.

In late 2008, the Dunhuang Academy established the Dunhuang Mogao Caves Conservation and Utilization Project Team. Fan Jinshi was the team leader, CPC committee secretary Ji Xinmin was in charge of supervision, executive vice president Wang Xudong was the general director of the engineering command, and vice president Luo Huaqing was in charge of digital program production. Under the leading group of the project, there was a monitoring group and a project command. The project command implemented the management of the construction project in strict accordance with the construction procedures stipulated by the State, implemented the project legal person responsibility system, project supervision system and bidding system, and strictly controlled the construction standard and total investment. President Fan Jinshi spared no effort, organized project bidding, research and demonstration, consulted domestic and foreign experts, learned engineering management methods and experience, and comprehensively coordinated the implementation of the project.

First, the site for the construction. The original concept for the Mogao Caves Digital Exhibition Center (hereafter Digital Exhibition Center) was to be built within the Mogao Caves Reserve, so that digital displays and cave visits could be placed close together for ease of management and tourist access. In 2006, Dunhuang Academy commissioned Lanzhou University to assess the environmental impact of the project. According to the assessment, the planned digital display facilities would have little impact on the Mogao Caves landscape,

Exterior view of Mogao Caves Digital Exhibition Center (photo by Wu Jian)

but the visitor reception facilities and ancillary facilities would significantly increase the environmental pressure on the Caves and be detrimental to the fragile ecological environment. The evaluation team recommended that to protect the natural landscape of the Mogao Caves in its entirety and authenticity, and to reduce human interference and pressure, the display and service facilities be relocated outside the Mogao Caves Reserve. Fan Jinshi paid great attention to this recommendation, and after several discussions, the final site was set south of the provincial Highway 314, which was 15 kilograms from the Magao Caves. In April 2007, the State Environmental Protection Administration approved the new site, giving it high recognition. After the official operation of the Digital Exhibition Center, it also assumed the role of digitally displaying Dunhuang culture and art, managing tourist flows, and offering places for parking, shopping, eating, etc., significantly reducing the environmental pressure on the Mogao Caves Reserve. In retrospect, the original site selection was a wise one.

Second, the design of the building. After bidding, Mr. Cui Kai, a master architect of the China Academy of Architecture and Design and an academician of the Chinese Academy of Engineering, was finally commissioned to design the Digital Exhibition Center. Mr. Cui Kai innovatively integrated the exquisite lines of Dunhuang art and the Gobi Desert into the design. The whole building resembles a flowing dune and the skirt of Apsaras, which grows out of the earth in a quicksand-like form, magnificent and unsophisticated, harmoniously blending with the desert and the surrounding environment. The interior design of the building includes a visitor reception hall, a dome theater, a digital cinema, a VIP reception hall and shopping, dining and office areas for visitors, providing a comfortable space for visitors while perfectly combining the space of four digital cinema halls. The whole building covers an area of about 100,000 square meters, with a construction area of 11,800 square meters.

Third, the construction of the project. The appearance of the Digital Exhibition Center building is undulating and varied, and the internal structure is also very complex, especially the two domed theaters. The diameter of the shell reaches 35 meters, and the whole body is composed of curved reinforced concrete. The installation of the ball grid frame, the exhaust ventilation in the hall, the fire alarm, and other works mean that this is among the world's most complex construction projects. Following bidding, the First Construction Engineering Group Co. Ltd of Guangxi Construction constructed the project, and the Gansu Seventh Construction Group Co. Ltd carried out the interior construction and decoration.

To ensure the construction quality and smooth the progress of the project, Fan Jinshi took over the project management herself. On the one hand, she strictly controlled the project, requiring that the construction be completed by the First Construction Engineering Group Co. Ltd of Guangxi Construction from the beginning to the end, and she successfully prevented the project from "being subcontracted layer by layer," thus avoiding lowering the quality of the project. On the other hand, with strict discipline, she took measures to prevent unscrupulous behavior that sometimes could occur in construction projects, to ensure that this project was "clean." With the increasing difficulty of the construction, the increase in the price of materials, and two consecutive years affected by floods, the shortage of funds for the later construction was over 100 million yuan. Fan Jinshi sought help from cultural lovers at home and abroad to raise money and funds. After several reports and requests, the National Development and Reform Commission and Gansu Province gave an additional investment of nearly 200 million yuan. The project was finally completed with the support of the government and the help of people from all walks of life at home and abroad, with perseverance and strict project management of the contractors.

Fourth, the program and its production. To display the exquisite murals of the Mogao Caves in high quality, Chen Jianjun, the director of China's first Dolby Digital Stereo recording film and the producer of CCTV documentary programs, was hired as the chief director and producer of the program. After numerous discussions with experts, scholars and creators, it was determined that the 8K ultra-high-definition dome-screen film *Fantasy Buddha Palace* should utilize the unique spatial shape of the dome to present the exquisite digitized cave murals in a way close to the natural caves in the form of artistic expression of film. The film is a 20-minute-long panoramic view of Cave 285, Cave 420, Cave 220, Cave 45, Cave 130 and other caves in the Mogao Caves Complex. The 4K high-definition widescreen film, *Millennium Mogao,* displays Dunhuang from the perspective of the history of human civilization and uses moving images to present the history of the Mogao Caves for more than 1,600 years, allowing the audience to fully experience the enormous historical and cultural values.

The dome-screen film Fantasy Buddha Palace *in the Mogao Caves Digital Exhibition Center (photo by Ding Xiaosheng)*

144

Film production was also quite complex, especially the dome film production. The technology used for the dome film was an "immersive new medium," until then, it was used primarily in science and technology museums and planetariums to show astronomy programs. This was the first time in the world that it had been used for cultural heritage. The program was also produced using several conventional techniques, including aerial surveying, archaeological mapping, laser scanning, reverse engineering and film modeling. Nearly 40 technicians worked 12 hours a day for seven months to obtain the data for the computer alone. The post-production process was also tricky, and although the film was only 20 minutes long, it took a professional team of nearly 100 people over four years to create and produce it.

Proposals to Achieve: A Balance Between Conservation and Utilization of Mogao Caves

In September 2014, the Mogao Caves Digital Exhibition Center was officially completed and began operations. Digital Exhibition Center's completion changed the pattern of tourist visits: one can enjoy a 45-minute digital movie and a 75-minute site visit into the Mogao Caves, instead of an average two-hour site visit in the past.

The new model reduces the time visitors spend at Mogao Caves by 45 minutes, and the maximum daily visitor capacity at Mogao Caves can be increased from 3,000 to 6,000. It not only reduces the pressure on the caves, but also enriches the visitors' experience and their knowledge of culture and art, achieving a win-win situation for the conservation and utilization of cultural relics.

The Mogao Caves Digital Exhibition Center is a successful attempt to achieve a deeper integration of technology and culture and to promote a balanced development model of preserving world cultural heritage and developing tourism. The Dunhuang Academy's model of openness, featuring "general control, online reservation, digital display, and on-site viewing of the caves," has also been emulated and promoted, providing experience and lessons for cultural heritage institutions around the world to explore the effective conservation and scientific utilization of cultural relics.

The "Proposal for the Construction of the Dunhuang Mogao Caves Visitor Center" has been listed as an excellent proposal of the 10th CPPCC National Committee and one of the 100 Influential and Important Proposals since the founding of the People's Republic of China. Looking back on the whole process from the conception to the implementation of the proposal, the most crucial factor is the high level of involvement by the government, with the full support and vigorous promotion of the CPPCC. In the process of proposal processing and project decision-making, the project's contractors and organizing departments always focused on the overall development of the CPC and the country, attached great importance to actively doing an excellent job in handling CPPCC proposals, so that the issues reflected in the proposal could obtain a timely response and quality solutions. Those departments include the Gansu Provincial Development and Reform Commission, Gansu Provincial Bureau of Cultural Heritage, and many central ministries and commissions such as the National Development and Reform Commission (NDRC), Ministry of Finance, Ministry of Science and Technology (MOST), National Cultural Heritage Administration (NCHA), State Environmental Protection Administration. All these processes vividly reflect the unique advantages, distinctive features and essential role of the CPPCC, as a vital carrier of socialist consultative democracy, in promoting socialist democratic politics with Chinese characteristics and participating in political affairs, democratic supervision and building a harmonious socialist society.

(Contributed by Dunhuang Academy)

The Proposal to Attach Great Importance to the Protection of Beijing-Hangzhou Grand Canal and Launch the World Heritage Site Application

14

PROFILE OF THE PRINCIPAL PROPOSER

LIU FENG, born in February 1937, is a native of Longyao, Hebei Province. He joined the CPC in August 1961, and started to work in August 1961 after graduating from Renmin University of China, with a BA in journalism. He was the chairman of the 6th CPPCC of Qinghai Province and the 7th and 8th CPPCC of Zhejiang Province. He was a delegate to the CPC's 13th, 14th and 15th National Congresses, and a member of the 7th to 10th CPPCC National Committee.

Story of the Proposal for World Heritage Status

On June 22, 2014, at the 38th Session of the World Heritage Committee held in Doha, Qatar, China's Grand Canal was successfully inscribed on the World Heritage List, following an eight-year-long application process. During this period, the CPPCC National Committee and the relevant provincial and municipal governments did a lot of fruitful work, such as members' proposals, specific researches, speeches at the General Assembly, collective interviews at the two sessions (the annual NPC and CPPCC sessions), holding summit forums, compiling a series of publications, etc., to make active proposals, coordinate all parties and build consensus. All this played a significant role in promoting the protection and recognition of the importance of the Grand Canal, and has become one of the highlights of the achievements of the CPPCC in performing its duties in the past 70 years.

Origin of the Application for the World Heritage Status

The story began with a commemorative symposium organized by the CPPCC National Committee in 2005. In 1985, Hou Renzhi, Yang Hanxi, Zheng Xiaoxie and Luo Zhewen, members of the 6th CPPCC National Committee, jointly proposed that China should join the UNESCO Convention Concerning the Protection of the World Cultural and Natural Heritage (hereafter the Convention). After the proposal was submitted, it received great attention from all parties. In November of that year, the 13th Session of the Standing Committee of the 6th

NPC decided to approve China's accession to the Convention, which opened the way for China's world heritage conservation. The year 2005 happened to be the 20th anniversary of China's accession to the Convention. On December 22, 2005, the Committee on Culture, Historical Data and Studies of the CPPCC, in conjunction with the National Commission of the People's Republic of China for UNESCO, the Ministry of Construction, the State Administration of Cultural Heritage, and the *CPPCC Daily* held a symposium in the auditorium of the CPPCC National Committee on "China's World Heritage Conservation after 20 Years." Mr. Zheng Xiaoxie, 90, Mr. Yang Hanxi, 87, and Mr. Luo Zhewen, 82, all attended. (Mr. Hou Renzhi, 95, delegated his eldest son Hou Fangxing to attend because of his old age) The experts gathered to plan for the protection of the World Heritage sites.

At the symposium, Mr. Luo Zhewen was positive that China ranked third in the world with 31 World Heritage sites. In addition to the efforts of the Ministry of Culture, the Ministry of Construction, the State Administration of Cultural Heritage and relevant departments, the active promotion of the CPPCC National Committee played a key role in reaching this outstanding achievement. He said that if our country had not participated in the Convention at the time or later, achieving such results would have been difficult today. In particular, he said, the Grand Canal culture was rich in its connotations and of great value. In the face of the ongoing South-to-North Water Diversion Project, the application for World Heritage status safeguarded the Grand Canal's conservation. He revealed that a few days ago, he, Mr. Zheng Xiaoxie and Zhu Bingren, a master of arts and crafts from Hangzhou, wrote a letter to the mayors of 18 cities along the Canal, calling for innovative ideas to speed up the process of the World Heritage Site application of the Beijing-Hangzhou Grand Canal. Luo said that the Great Wall had been inscribed on the World Heritage List in 1987, but the Grand Canal had not been associated with World Heritage for various reasons. The CPPCC National Committee had done a lot of work in promoting the protection of cultural heritage and hoped that the Committee on Culture, Historical Data and Studies would play a role in the World Heritage Site application of the Beijing-Hangzhou Grand Canal.

The letter mentioned by Mr. Luo Zhewen was sent in December 2005, when he and Mr. Zheng went to Hangzhou to attend a symposium on the planning of the West Lake scenic area. After 20 years of World Heritage protection in China, it became their common wish and responsibility to win the honor of World Culture Heritage for the Grand Canal. The letter reads: "Coming down through history, the value and inheritance of the Beijing-Hangzhou Grand Canal must not be 'cut off' in the hands of our generation .... We have every reason to believe that through the application, the Beijing-Hangzhou Grand Canal can completely form a new cultural and natural landscape belt with Chinese characteristics; while protecting and promoting the millennium-old Chinese culture, it can also make the life of people along the Beijing-Hangzhou Grand Canal better."

Conceive a Topic

After the symposium, the meeting of the directors of the Committee on Culture, Historical Data and Studies took the "Preservation of Historical Relics along the Canal" as an alternative topic for the Committee's research in 2006. In early January 2006, at the plenary session of the Committee on Culture, Historical Data and Studies, the members showed great interest in the topic of the Grand Canal. After a heated discussion, "Protection and World Heritage Site Application of the Grand Canal" was determined as the annual key research topic. In February, the committee office invited Luo Zhewen and Xie Chensheng to be guests of the CPPCC, and asked the two old members for advice on how to carry out the work. Luo said, the Grand Canal heritage involved many provinces, cities, and departments. Among 18 canal cities, only the city leaders of Hangzhou and Yangzhou had given feedback on the letter of the application for World Cultural Heritage, and the most important thing at present was to draw the attention of the leadership and society as a whole. He proposed to follow the example of China's joining the World Heritage Convention, that the CPPCC members presenting the idea to the relevant departments jointly, and then organizing larger-scale research activities, effectively publicizing through the media, and reporting the results of the research to the central government.

At this time, Liu Feng, former chairman of the Zhejiang Provincial Committee of the CPPCC and then deputy director of the Committee on Culture, Historical Data and Studies of the CPPCC, who was working and living in Hangzhou, was also very concerned about the Canal. He repeatedly investigated the achievements of Hangzhou in the protection and improvement of the Canal, and proposed to make the Hangzhou section of the Grand Canal a "new cultural highlight and a new cultural brand" in Hangzhou. In early 2002, the Ninth Party Congress of Hangzhou made the decision to implement the comprehensive improvement, protection and development project of the Canal (Hangzhou section), and set up a corresponding organization to focus on the three primary goals of "returning the Canal to the people, creating world-class tourism products, and applying for World Heritage status." Hangzhou was also the city that initiated the Grand Canal Cultural Festival.

On the eve of the two sessions in 2006, Liu Feng convened a symposium at the CPPCC, attended by more than ten people, including Yu Rongren, then a member of the CPPCC National Committee and chairman of the Hangzhou CPPCC, and comrades in charge of the Office of the Committee on Culture, Historical Data and Studies and the Hangzhou Municipal Government. They mentioned that the Grand Canal protection and heritage application was a multifaceted project, involving culture, cultural relics, construction, water conservancy, transportation, environmental protection, and other relevant ministries and dozens of cities along the Canal, so it needed a unified approach and a concerted effort to give adequate protection to the Grand Canal to achieve the success of the application. The CPPCC should exploit its advantages, do in-depth research, and create a great deal of momentum to draw the attention and support of society to the Grand Canal protection and World Heritage Site application.

Several things were agreed at the meeting: First, Liu Feng took the lead in submitting a proposal on the protection and the World Heritage Site application of the Beijing-Hangzhou Grand Canal, calling for starting the work at a national strategic level. Second, in mid-May, a full inspection of the Grand Canal should be organized, inviting a vice chairman of the CPPCC National Committee as the leader, and members of the Committee on Culture, Historical Data and Studies and experts in related fields, and the heads of the provincial and municipal associations along the Canal to attend. Third, after the inspection, a symposium would be held in Hangzhou, where the leaders of the CPPCC

National Committee would give speeches and the mayors of the cities along the Canal would be invited to participate.

Joint Proposal

On March 5, 2006, after the opening of the Fourth Session of the 10th CPPCC National Committee, comrades from the office of the Committee on Culture, Historical Data and Studies of the CPPCC submitted the first draft of the proposal, "Protection of Beijing-Hangzhou Grand Canal Should Be Given High Priority and the Application Should Be Launched," to Liu Feng. He revised some words and finalized it. On March 6, the proposal was distributed to the CPPCC members for comments and the plan to jointly submit the proposal was carried out in three locations. Liu Feng's group was composed of the then or former chairs of the provincial and municipal governments along the Grand Canal. The chairpersons strongly felt that the CPPCC's engagement in this topic was significant for protecting the Canal and economic development along the route. They gave their active support to the proposal. Other comrades from the office took the proposal to China Resources Hotel, where the social science, literature and arts circles was based and the committee members were more concentrated, and Zhongxie Hotel, where the press and publication circles was based, to solicit signatures respectively. The members showed great enthusiasm, and in just half a day the number of members who signed reached 58, which included Zhang Wenbin and Shan Jixiang, former directors of the National Cultural Heritage Administration, as well as Shu Yi, Wang Tiecheng, Wu Yanze and other cultural celebrities.

The proposal pointed out that, as a critical "water transport of grain to the capital" and a bridge for cultural exchange in ancient China, the Beijing-Hangzhou Grand Canal embodied huge amounts of information in many fields like politics, economy, culture, science and technology of China, and made significant contributions to China's economic and social development, national unification and social progress. The protection and the World Heritage Site application of the Beijing-Hangzhou Grand Canal was by no means a matter of one province, one place or one department, and it was by no means an unimportant matter, but a matter of sustainable development of the eastern part of China, the heritage of Chinese civilization and the protection of the natural ecological environment. The work of safeguarding and protecting the Beijing-Hangzhou Grand Canal should be started immediately at a strategic level, and the World Heritage Site application project should be started at an appropriate time. The proposal put forward five specific recommendations.

First, a unified and coordinated mechanism should be established, leading by the leaders of the State Council. It is to organize relevant departments, provinces and cities to plan and implement the protection and application, and make decisions on important issues.

Second, a research institution should be set up with the participation and support of relevant ministries and commissions, relevant experts, and governments along the Canal to conduct investigation, research and value assessment, ascertain the essential details of the Grand Canal, especially the "landscape" and intangible culture as the focus of the collection of information, and put forward feasible proposals.

Third, under the guidance of the scientific outlook on development, the overall protection plan for the Grand Canal should be formulated as soon as possible, and there should be proper handling of the relationship between protection, remediation and development and the relationship with the South-to-North Water Diversion Project should be handled appropriately, to provide the basis for the remediation around the Canal.

Fourth, according to the requirements of the Convention Concerning the Protection of the World Cultural and Natural Heritage and requirements of the World Heritage Site application, it should take the application for the status of both the natural and cultural heritage and the intangible cultural heritage into account. The introduction about the sites should be innovative, so as to elaborate on their unique and important heritage value, and strive for formal application in the next five years.

Fifth, the unified identification of the Beijing-Hangzhou Grand Canal Heritage should be collected and released.

The proposal stated: "We have reason to believe that the Grand Canal and the Great Wall should be 'sisters' on the heritage list, and the former is more dynamic, charming, and characteristic." On March 10, 2006, Xinhua News Agency published a circular article "Beijing-Hangzhou Grand Canal Is Comparable to the Great Wall: CPPCC Members Call for 'Safeguarding and Protection,'" reporting this joint proposal, which immediately became a highly reported topic by major media.

Trip in May

After the closing of the two sessions, the National Committee of the CPPCC began preparations for a full-scale study tour of the Grand Canal and a symposium in Hangzhou. The number of the Committee on Culture, Historical Data and Studies members who signed up for the study tour was larger than that for any previous tour, and many members canceled or postponed their other activities in May to walk the "river of history and culture." The final composition of the delegation was 68 people, including 23 CPPCC members, 11 well-known experts and scholars in various fields, 14 journalists from the central news agencies, and comrades in charge of the history and literature committees of the six provinces and municipalities along the Canal. Chen Kuiyuan, then vice chairman of the CPPCC National Committee worked as the head of the delegation, and Liu Feng and Cheng Shi'e, then deputy directors of the Committee on Culture, Historical Data and Studies of the CPPCC, as deputy heads.

On May 12, 2006, the "Beijing-Hangzhou Grand Canal Protection and the World Heritage Site Application Campaign Launching Ceremony" was held in the first-floor hall of the Capital Museum. Liu Qi, then a member of the Political Bureau of the Central Committee of the CPC and secretary of the Beijing Municipal Committee, and Chen Kuiyuan, then vice chairman of the National Committee of the CPPCC and head of the delegation, delivered warm speeches and unveiled the commemorative logo for the campaign. The logo is shaped by an oar placed diagonally across the seal, symbolizing that the working people were and still are the creators of the Canal's long history and splendid culture. The designer is Zhu Bingren, a master of Chinese arts and crafts.

The afternoon before the launch ceremony, the delegation member Mr. Zheng Xiaoxie was interviewed by the press at his home. Perhaps he got too

In May 2006, the delegation of Beijing-Hangzhou Grand Canal Protection and the World Heritage Site Application of the CPPCC National Committee visited the Tianjin section of the Beijing-Hangzhou Grand Canal

excited. Soon after the interview, he felt ill, and was sent to the hospital. His first words after regaining consciousness after a night of emergency treatment in the ICU were, "I need to go to Tianjin!" Only after everyone dissuaded him did Zheng give up the trip. Entrusted by the Committee on Culture, Historical Data and Studies of the CPPCC, Zheng and Luo visited Hangzhou and Yangzhou from March 17 to 22, despite their old age, to find a solution for the protection of the Grand Canal and its application for World Cultural Heritage status. Mr. Zhu Bingren recalled that as soon as Zheng set foot on Hangzhou's Gongchen Bridge, he said with deep emotion, "Old friend, I'm here to see you again!" His sincerity was touching.

On the eve of departure, another member of the delegation, veteran member Mr. Luo Zhewen, was riding a bicycle in the district when the pedal suddenly broke. He fell off the bike and hurt his knee. On the first half of the trip, Mr. Luo walked with a limp due to his leg injuries. He was advised to rest more, but Luo always waved his hand, smiled and said, "It's okay!" On several occasions on the boat, he pulled up his trouser legs to dry his wounds.

Mr. Chen Qiaoyi, 84, a tenured professor at Zhejiang University, is a great researcher in the history of water conservancy, and he is a stubborn and respectable old gentleman. Wherever he went, Mr. Chen always asked for detailed data, and from occasionally, he exchanged a few words with the comrades who introduced the situation; when he was in a hurry, he spoke directly in English. The 85-year-old famous cultural relics conservation expert Mr. Xie Chensheng also climbed slopes and waded through ditches despite his old age.

At the beginning of the study tour, Dong Biwu's daughter, Dong Lianghui, fell and injured her ankle. When they traveled to Tianjin, her injury was severe, but she insisted on walking the whole journey, and declined the local escort's advice to use a wheelchair several times. On the second half of the journey, her foot injury was much better. She walked with the help of a cane, walking in the expedition, resembling her father Dong Biwu.

There were touching stories about the study tour every day. The spirit of these members and experts, who took responsibility for retaining the roots of historical and cultural heritage, went out of their way and traveled far and wide to infect every young reporter and every young staff member with their enthusiasm.

After 10 days, the delegation arrived at Hangzhou at noon on May 21, having traveled more than 2,500 kilometers, visiting 18 cities and more than 30 counties in 6 provinces in various canal sections, harvesting abundant first-hand information. The delegation received a warm welcome from the provincial and municipal parties and government leaders and people along the route. Zhang Lichang, then a member of the Political Bureau of the Central Committee of the CPC and secretary of the Tianjin Municipal Committee, Xi Jinping, then secretary of the Zhejiang Provincial Committee, Lü Zushan, then governor of Zhejiang Province, and the chairpersons of the CPPCC of Tianjin, Shandong, Jiangsu and Zhejiang provinces were there to meet all members of the delegation. Each city's municipal committee secretary and mayor accompanied the delegation and introduced the situation. The 14 journalists accompanying the delegation were from the central and Hangzhou news agencies. Because of the tight schedule, the daily work was full and intense. It was early summer, and the weather was sultry. The reporters were still working tirelessly. Over more than ten days, *People's Daily* Online, *CPPCC Daily*, Hangzhou TV, *Qianjiang Evening News* and other media gave daily special reports.

Hangzhou Declaration

On May 22, the Beijing-Hangzhou Grand Canal Protection and the World Heritage Site Application symposium was grandly held in Hangzhou. Nearly 200 people attended, including members of the delegation, comrades in charge of relevant ministries and commissions, vice chairmen in charge of the CPPCC of six provinces (or municipalities directly under the central government), mayors or vice mayors in charge of 18 cities, as well as the chairpersons of the CPPCC of these cities. Dozens of media reporters followed along and gathered in Hangzhou.

At the symposium, Vice Chairman Chen Kuiyuan gave a speech. Main leaders of 18 cities introduced the situation of the canal section and the conservation work in their respective cities. The members and experts combined their findings from the visit. They elaborated on how to successfully protect the Grand Canal and make a successful World Heritage status application from the perspective of their respective research fields. Shan Jixiang, then a member of the CPPCC National Committee and head of the National Cultural Heritage Administration, was ill but attended all the activities in Hangzhou despite his illness and made an important speech at the closing session. He had been involved with the Grand Canal and its cultural heritage since 2003, and submitted several related proposals.

The most important result achieved at the meeting was the adoption of the Hangzhou Declaration on the Protection and World Heritage Site Application of the Beijing-Hangzhou Grand Canal. The declaration pointed out that the Beijing-Hangzhou Grand Canal was a great project created by the ancient working people of China, a precious material and spiritual treasure left to us by our ancestors, and an important living human heritage. In the course of more than two thousand years of history, the Grand Canal made important contributions to China's economic development, national unification, social progress and cultural prosperity, and still plays a significant role today. Protecting the Beijing-Hangzhou Grand Canal is vital for passing on human civilization and promoting harmonious social development.

The declaration proposed that, with the development of economy and society, the traditional transport function of the Grand Canal had changed, the Canal, the landscape and people's lives along the Canal had changed greatly, and the Canal was currently facing severe challenges of both urban and rural modernization and construction. If we did not strengthen its protection, the Grand Canal's historical and cultural heritage, scenery and natural ecological environment would inevitably be destroyed, and its authenticity and integrity would no longer exist, which would be a substantial irreparable loss for the Chinese nation. The safeguarding, protection and sustainable development of the Grand Canal had reached a critical juncture.

The declaration calls for raising public social awareness of the important status and multiple values of the Grand Canal, further enhancing the conservation awareness of governments at all levels, and mobilizing the whole of society to participate in the conservation and World Heritage Site application of the Grand Canal. We should implement the scientific outlook on development, pay more attention to the overall appearance of the Grand Canal in the planning and implementation of economic and social development along it, ensure the effective protection of cultural relics along the route, rationalize the use of resources, maintain the ecological environment, achieve sustainable development, and effectively turn the process of "application" into a process of strengthening the protection and management of the Grand Canal, so as to sustain the cultural heritage of the Canal.

Re-creation of the Climax

The year 2006 was destined to be the year of the Grand Canal. On May 25, the day after the symposium, the State Council announced the Beijing-Hangzhou Grand Canal as the "Sixth Group of Key Cultural Heritage Sites under State Protection," and in October, the Third Grand Canal Cultural Festival and Summit Forum on Protection and Heritage Application was held in Tongzhou District, Beijing. In November, the Committee on Culture, Historical Data and

Studies of the CPPCC and the Beijing Municipal Committee of the CPPCC jointly organized the first exhibition of a huge long horizontal traditional Chinese painting entitled "The Ancient Canal: Looking Back." At the same time, the provincial and municipal governments along the Canal held various activities to offer advice and suggestions for the application. With the deepening of understanding, the concept of the Grand Canal gradually expanded from the "Beijing-Hangzhou Grand Canal" to the "Grand Canal of China," including the Sui-Tang Grand Canal and the Eastern Zhejiang Canal. On December 15, 2006, the State Administration of Cultural Heritage announced "China's World Heritage Preliminary List," in which the Grand Canal ranked first, involving eight provinces and 35 cities.

At the end of January 2007, the Committee on Culture, Historical Data and Studies of the CPPCC submitted to the Central Committee a research report "Suggestions on the Protection and the World Heritage Site Application of the Grand Canal." The report made suggestions in six areas: First, guide the protection, utilization and World Heritage Site application of the Grand Canal with a scientific outlook on its development; second, attach great importance to the preservation and application of the Grand Canal as considered from a national strategic level; third, formulate and introduce the "Regulations on the Protection of the Grand Canal"; fourth, do the basic work on the protection and application of the Grand Canal; fifth, consider both the protection of the cultural heritage and ecological environment of the Grand Canal and the east route of the South-to-North Water Diversion Project; sixth, mobilize the whole of society to participate in the protection and World Heritage Site application of the Grand Canal.

On March 11, 2007, Liu Feng, on behalf of the Committee on Culture, Historical Data and Studies of the CPPCC, made a speech on "Attaching Great Importance to the Protection and the World Heritage Site Application of the Beijing-Hangzhou Grand Canal" at the Fifth Session of the 10th CPPCC National Committee. The then State Councilor Chen Zhili immediately approved that the proposal on the protection and World Heritage Site application of the Beijing-Hangzhou Grand Canal deserved great attention. "Please make an analysis and do the work that can be done first, and the long-term, extensive problems can be solved afterwards with in-depth research and feasibility studies," Chen said.

On the afternoon of the same day, the General Assembly News Team in the Great Hall of the People (Hebei Hall) specially arranged a group interview, and invited Liu Feng, Shan Jixiang, Shu Yi, Liu Qingzhu to introduce the situation and answer reporters' questions. The media was enthusiastic, the hall was almost full, and the interactive atmosphere was warm. Behind the banner hanging above the four members was a huge oil painting depicting the Jinshanling Great Wall. What a coincidence! As two great projects in ancient China, the Grand Canal and the Great Wall are both symbols of the cultural identity of the Chinese nation. We should protect the Grand Canal and the Great Wall, and this is our unavoidable responsibility and glorious mission.

On March 11, 2007, the Fifth Session of the 10th CPPCC National Committee held a collective interview on protecting the Beijing Hangzhou Grand Canal and the World Heritage Application. From left to right are: Li Renchen, Liu Feng, Shan Jixiang, Shu Yi, and Liu Qingzhu.

Continued Effort

The Beijing-Hangzhou Grand Canal National Cultural Park is, first and foremost, a park. However, it is different from an ordinary citizen's park. It is a public space integrating past and present, culture and tourism, life and leisure, knowledge and emotion, and nature and humanity. The park is a public place that everyone can freely enter and experience. Moreover, this park serves not only tourists, but all those who are associated with the Grand Canal along its route. It is a beautiful part of the melody of life and will form a wonderful part of people's collective memory in the future.

Moreover, the Beijing-Hangzhou Grand Canal National Cultural Park is all about culture. The cultural heritage of the Grand Canal is like a river flowing through time, carrying the essence of culture condensed in history. Showcasing the relics continuously breathes new life into the cultural heritage. Culture is not only historical knowledge or legendary stories. It is internalized in the blood of a nation. The culture created and nourished by the Grand Canal, which has been flowing for more than 2,000 years, has shaped the way Chinese people see themselves and the world today, and the spirit and wisdom of self-improvement, eclecticism, openness, tolerance and harmonious co-existence are preserved and recounted through the Grand Canal National Cultural Park.

The most important thing about the Grand Canal National Cultural Park is that it belongs to the whole country. This is not the amusement park of a city or a township, nor is it the property of a governmental department; it is a huge national project that runs through Beijing to Hangzhou, containing one river section and 34 prefecture-level cities in nine provinces, with 410 million people. It is also a system to which many ministries and industries are committed. Historically, the Grand Canal itself was the manifestation of the national will and the unity of the country. Today, the Grand Canal is the embodiment of thousands of years of Chinese history, excellent traditional culture, great contemporary spirit and strong cultural confidence. Such a national cultural park allows everyone involved to feel the country's power and the enduring vitality of Chinese civilization. Whether walking next to the waters of the Canal, enjoying the cultural heritage, feeling the pulse of the Canal's history, or using technology understand its history better, this park conveys Chinese values and shapes Chinese identity.

The Grand Canal is a canal of eternal love. CPPCC people have a historical responsibility for the Grand Canal that they cannot relinquish, and it has been a great success story.

From the Fifth to the Tenth Session of the CPPCC National Committee, along the route of the Canal study tour, there had been a whole series of research sites and proposals, all part of the painstaking process of application for the World Heritage status. These have harvested fruitful results and left a string of "flashing footprints."

Since the 10th to the 13th CPPCC National Committee, another 15 winters and springs have come and gone. No matter how the times develop and change, the CPPCC people who love the Grand Canal will not lose their passion.

When willows on the Canal banks swayed in the spring breezes of 2017, General Secretary Xi Jinping proposed to fully explore the rich historical and cultural resources of the Grand Canal, and protect and utilize the Grand Canal, a valuable heritage left to us by our ancestors. On this occasion, the construction of the Grand Canal Cultural Belt was placed on the important agenda of the Central Committee of the CPC, which has put this work into the fast lane of the New Era and entering a new stage of innovative development.

With General Secretary Xi Jinping's important instructions to study and explore new ways and means to protect and manage the Canal, the CPPCC members stood on the threshold of the New Era and put forward many constructive, insightful proposals. CPPCC leaders, relevant departments and members joined hands to retake the Canal road again, go deep into the front line, carrying out multi-level, multi-faceted field research, continuing to enrich and expand their "Canal achievements."

In the spring of the 70th birthday of the Republic, the CPPCC National Committee held a fortnightly consultation forum on "Promoting the Construction of the Grand Canal Cultural Belt." This was the re-learning of Xi Jinping's thought of socialism with Chinese characteristics in the New Era, and the re-examination of the major issue of the Grand Canal culture heritage, protection, and utilization, as well as the practice of the new development concept and the recommencement of discussion by CPPCC members who love the Grand Canal. Twelve members, experts and scholars gave speeches and opinions on promoting the construction of the Grand Canal Cultural Belt. Ninety-eight members of the CPPCC spoke enthusiastically on the mobile platform where CPPCC members could perform their duties. Wang Yang, a member of the Standing Committee of the Political Bureau of the Central Committee of the CPC, then chairman of the CPPCC National Committee, presided over the meeting and made a speech. He stressed that constructing the Grand Canal Cultural Belt was a thousand-year project, worthy of every effort of CPPCC members. We should establish cultural self-awareness and firm our cultural self-confidence, constantly emphasizing protection rather than large-scale development during the construction of the Grand Canal Cultural Belt to showcase Chinese civilization and make it an iconic cultural brand for national rejuvenation.

(Contributed by Wang Wenyun, Director of the First Editorial Office of the China Literature and History Publishing House)

The Proposal on Actively Responding to Regional Haze Pollution

15

PROFILE OF THE PROPOSER

The Chinese Peasants and Workers Democratic Party (CPWDP) mainly comprises intellectuals in medicine and health, population resources, and ecological environment.

The previous leaders and chairpersons of the CPWDP were Deng Yanda, Huang Qixiang, Zhang Bojun, Ji Fang, Zhou Gucheng, Lu Jiaxi, Jiang Zhenghua, and Sang Guowei. The current chairman is Chen Zhu.

As of June 2017, the total number of the CPWDP members was 157,000.

Actively Responding to Regional Haze Pollution to Safeguard People's Health Rights and Interests

On September 10, 2013, the Action Plan on Prevention and Control of Air Pollution (hereafter "Plan"), perhaps the most effective environmental policy in China in the past few years, was officially issued. The main goals set at that time were: By working hard over the next five years, air quality would be improved, and severe air pollution would be significantly reduced; the air quality in Beijing-Tianjin-Hebei, Yangtze River Delta, Pearl River Delta, and other regions would be improved significantly. We would also strive to clean heavily polluted air and significantly improve air quality across the country in another five or more years. In particular, it was clear that by 2017, the concentration ratio of inhalable particulate matter in cities at the prefecture level and above nationwide would have dropped by more than 10% compared with 2012; that of delicate particulate matter in Beijing-Tianjin-Hebei, Yangtze River Delta, Pearl River Delta would have dropped by 25%, 20%, and 15% respectively. The annual average concentration of delicate particulate matter in Beijing would have been controlled at about 60 micrograms per cubic meter. The introduction of this Plan was the start of air pollution control and laid the foundation for the later revision of the Law of the People's Republic of China on the Prevention and Control of Atmospheric Pollution.

The introduction of this major policy was the result of the painstaking efforts of members of the CPWDP, whose Central Committee carried out extensive and in-depth research, and put forward intensive and combined proposals. Among these proposals there was the "Proposal on Actively Responding to Regional Haze Pollution" submitted to the First Session of the 12th CPPCC National Committee in the name of the Central Committee of CPWDP.

Focus on Environment and Health

When General Secretary Xi Jinping visited the Central Committee of the CPWDP, the leading body of the 15th Central Committee of the CPWDP stated that they should lead all the CPWDP members further to give rein to the advantages of the CPWDP, and take the development goals of "Healthy China" and "Beautiful China" as the main ways to improve people's health. The intersection of environment and health should be the starting point and focus of the CPWDP's political participation.

At the beginning of the 21st century, although China's economy developed rapidly, the development strategy we adopted to propelled economic growth, but neglected the environment, thus putting enormous pressure on the environment. The beginning of 2013 witnessed successive large-scale haze pollution incidents in China, seriously affecting public health and social order. On January 17, the Central Committee of the CPWDP went to Guangzhou to carry out the CPC history education activities. At that time, the haze pollution was in its most serious period. On the high-speed train from Beijing to Guangzhou, members from the Central Committee of the CPWDP saw that haze pollution was severe in North China. The visibility was reduced (only tens of meters in some places), air quality was degraded, and travel and public health were seriously affected. What they saw highlighted the importance of air pollution control. On January 22, Wang Jinnan, then a member of the Standing Committee of the CPWDP Central Committee and deputy director of the Environmental Planning Research Institute of the Ministry of Environmental Protection, submitted the "Suggestions on Immediately Carrying out Health Damage Assessment of Haze Pollution" to the Central Committee of the CPWDP. Chairman Chen Zhu attached great importance to Wang's report. He said that if not handled properly, the problem would have a far-reaching and significant negative impact on China's economic and social development, and even affect the leadership of the CPC and the credibility of the government, making it difficult to achieve the development goals of a "Beautiful China" and "Healthy China." He gave instructions and strategic guidance, made arrangements for handling the problem, recommended that investigations be carried out into the relationship between the environment and public health, and suggested comprehensive management of the issue.

Conducting Scientific and In-depth Researches and Discussions

Following Chairman Chen Zhu's instructions, upholding the principle of "comprehensiveness, truth, depth and feasibility," members of the Department of Political Participation and Deliberation under the leadership of He Wei, then vice chairman and secretary general of the Central Committee of the CPWDP, carried out detailed and in-depth investigations and researches in various forms.

First, symposiums, which relevant government departments attended, were organized to gain an overview of the issue. On February 5, 2013, Chairman Chen Zhu presided over an inter-departmental and interdisciplinary expert symposium. Leaders from the Ministry of Health, Ministry of Environmental Protection, Chinese Center for Disease Control and Prevention (China CDC), China Meteorological Administration and other departments, public health experts from Fudan University and doctors from Peking University Third Hospital and Beijing Chaoyang Hospital described the causes, harm and specific suggestions for tackling regional haze pollution from the following perspectives: meteorology, ecological environment, and population health. Vice Chairman He Wei made specific instructions about proposing suggestions on this issue. After the meeting, the Central Committee of the CPWDP collected first-hand information on haze pollution in Beijing, Shijiazhuang, Chengdu, Guangzhou and Shenyang through different channels. Second, the research group conducted in-depth research through visits and exclusive interviews, and experts discussed the causes of haze pollution and the roles of various pollutant particles in causing it. An official from the Ministry of Environmental Protection said to the research team: "If I don't present everything that I know about haze control, I will not have a good time during this Spring Festival." Third, the research group obtained authentic material through continuous collection of data. To get data on the damage to health caused by the London Smog Incident of 1952, the research team repeatedly communicated with the officials of China CDC to verify the evidence, and by reviewing numerous evaluation reports, they concluded that "the deaths of nearly 10,000 people were presumed to be related to the smog in the winter of 1952 in London." Fourth, the research group suggested practical strategies and feasible measures. He Wei said, "Our suggestions must be practical and feasible. Just like a doctor who must prescribe medicine that can cure a disease after diagnosing it, we must offer practical and feasible measures after investigating the problem." To this end, members from the Department of Political Affairs and Deliberation had in-depth discussions with experts, hoping to develop practical suggestions. At a symposium held later by the National Development and Reform Commission (NDRC), an official from the Ministry of Environmental Protection commented, "Every suggestion made by the Central Committee of the CPWDP is very pragmatic and highly practicable."

Equal Emphasis on the Timeliness of Discussion and the Effectiveness of Suggestions

Chairman Chen Zhu and other leaders from the Central Committee of the CPWDP were mostly expert leaders with governmental experience. They were well aware that it was urgent to control the haze, and they had repeatedly instructed to conduct in-depth research, urgently emphasizing both practicality and timeliness. He Wei, who was in charge of political participation and deliberation at that time, also stressed that we must respond quickly to major events in economic and social life, concentrate our efforts, conduct timely investigations, and provide information and suggestions as soon as possible. If time moved on and the situation changed, research results would be useless even if they were accurate and comprehensive. As the proposal was put forward by the Central Committee of the CPWDP on time, it attracted the attention of all parties and the leaders of the Central Committee of the CPC. The large-scale haze incidents occurred on January 10, 2013 and the Central Committee of the CPWDP decided to investigate the issue on January 17, which was only one week later. It took only 21 working days from the official launch of the investigation to the submission of the special report to General Secretary Xi Jinping on February 20.

On February 22, the Central Committee of the CPWDP submitted the "Proposal on Actively Responding to Regional Haze Pollution" to the First Session of the 12th CPPCC National Committee in advance. The proposal made the following suggestions: (1) coordinate the regional haze pollution control at the national level; (2) establish a multi-level responsibility system to provide a solid organizational guarantee for the prevention and control of haze pollution; (3) make painstaking efforts to control air pollution in key areas and launch special campaigns promptly; (4) strengthen planning guidance, improve relevant standards, and launch the National Air Quality and Public Health Protection Project; (5) counteract the negative influence of air pollution on public health by technology; (6) enhance public awareness of environmental protection and launch national actions. The proposal was listed as a key proposal of the CPPCC National Committee. During the session, the CPPCC National Committee also held a consultation meeting on the proposal entitled "Strengthen the Prevention and Control of Urban and Rural Pollution and Improve the Living Environment in Urban and Rural Areas." The proposal submitted by the Central Committee of the CPWDP to tackle haze pollution was among them, and He Wei once again spoke at the meeting. At the consultation, leaders from the NDRC, the Ministry of Industry and Information Technology, and the Ministry of Environmental Protection responded positively to the "Proposal on Actively Responding to Regional Haze Pollution." They communicated with the proposers on the following work and specific measures, and collected suggestions on refining relevant policies.

On March 7, He Wei delivered a speech entitled "Coping with Haze Pollution, Purifying the Skies over China, and Safeguarding People's Rights to Good Health" at the Second Plenary Meeting of the First Session of the 12th CPPCC National Committee, and this had a strong response from all walks of life. He Wei's speech represented the consensus of members in medicine and health, and in ecological and environmental protection. Although the speech lasted only eight minutes, it expressed the deep concern of the Central Committee and all members of the CPWDP about the deterioration of the environment and the damage to public health. The speech also attracted the attention of many mainstream media. "The four rounds of applause embodied a strong desire for, and recognition of the need for, the prevention and control of haze pollution," according to the Xinhua News Agency. "Two Sessions 1+1" on CCTV 13 also covered He Wei's speech with "shared breath" as its keyword. A reporter from Xinhua News Agency interviewed He Wei that evening and published "Behind the Proposal Is the Responsibility: Tracking of the Proposal by the Central Committee of the CPWDP to Control the Haze" on Xinhuanet, introducing the structure and points of the proposal in detail.

Introducing Major Policies Thanks to Joint Efforts by Many Ministries and Commissions

To implement the instructions of the leaders of the Central Committee of the CPC and to further strengthen the prevention and control of haze pollution, on March 21, 2013, the NDRC launched a symposium attended by more than 50 persons from over 30 relevant organizations. The NDRC attached great importance to "Proposals on Actively Responding to Regional Haze Pollution" and related proposals and conveyed instructions issued by leaders of the Central Committee of the CPC. An official from the Department of Political Participation and Deliberation of the Central Committee of the CPWDP emphasized in his speech that to tackle air pollution, due attention should be paid to the following aspects. First, strengthen the leadership and overall planning about haze control, and form a systematic responsibility system. Second, make painstaking efforts to tackle air pollution in key areas and launch a special campaign for air pollution control. Third, create a social climate in which everyone participates in tackling air pollution. The leaders of the NDRC said that the proposal by the Central Committee of the CPWDP not only presented long-term planning, strategic, and forward-looking suggestions but also considered the urgency and feasibility of haze control. It was a pleasure to see that many measures were highly feasible. Hopefully, the ties with the Central Committee of the CPWDP could be further strengthened; the role of this united front in haze control could be further enhanced; and the unique advantages of the democratic parties could be fully exploited to report relevant issues, lead and mobilize people and organizations in all areas to tackle the haze pollution together. Based on discussion with experts and investigation, suggestions on tackling haze pollution would be submitted to the Central Committee of the CPC and contribute to the realization of a "Beautiful China."

The direct results of this symposium were the formation of the basic principles of the Action Plan on Prevention and Control of Air Pollution. Half a year later, the Plan was officially promulgated and implemented, establishing a clear path for air pollution prevention and control in China and setting a new mechanism of government leadership and corporate governance driven by market forces and public participation. The year 2017 saw the successful end of the Plan, while campaigns against air pollution prevention and control continue in China. At the two sessions in 2017, Premier Li Keqiang stated in the Report on the Work of the Government that "we will make our skies blue again." On June 27, 2018, the State Council issued the Three-Year Action Plan to Fight Air Pollution, marking the transition from tackling symptoms to tackling both symptoms and root causes of air pollution in China. On October 26, 2018, the revision of the Law of the People's Republic of China on the Prevention and Control of Atmospheric Pollution came into effect, marking China's entry into a new stage of law-based pollution control. We believe that under the strong leadership of the Central Committee of the CPC with Xi Jinping at its core, as long as we adhere to the principle of co-management, preventing and controlling air pollution at the source, and continuously carrying out prevention and control actions, we will surely win victory in defending blue skies.

(Contributed by the Central Committee of the CPWDP)

No. 0001, the Second Session of the 9th CPPCC National Committee

The Proposal on Increasing Investment to Manage the Yellow River by the Law

16

PROFILE OF THE PROPOSER

The China Democratic League (CDL) comprises of qualified senior intellectuals engaged in work related to culture, education, or science and technology.

The previous successive chairs of the CDL were Huang Yanpei, Zhang Lan, Shen Junru, Yang Mingxuan, Shi Liang, Hu Yuzhi (acting chairman), Chu Tunan, Fei Xiaotong, Ding Shisun, Jiang Shusheng, and Zhang Baowen. The current chairman is Ding Zhongli.

As of October 2017, the CDL had established organizations in 30 provinces, autonomous regions, and municipalities with more than 288,000 members.

Protecting the Yellow River is a Long-term Plan Related to the Great Rejuvenation of the Chinese Nation

The year 1999 was remarkable. Countless people worldwide eagerly looked forward to the new century's rays of sunshine. The two sessions (the annual NPC and CPPCC sessions) that year coincided with the 50th anniversary of the founding of the People's Republic of China, which attracted people's attention more than ever. At the Second Session of the 9th CPPCC National Committee this year, the Central Committee of the CDL submitted a proposal entitled "Proposal on Increasing Investment to Manage the Yellow River by the Law." It was listed as the No. 1 proposal and became a highlight of the conference.

Immediately after the proposal was announced in the *People's Daily*, the *CPPCC Daily* and the *Henan Daily*, it became a hot topic during the two sessions. Later, the proposal was selected as one of the outstanding proposals of the 9th CPPCC National Committee and one of the "Important and Influential Proposals of the CPPCC National Committee since Its Establishment 70 Years Ago." Looking back on this issue 20 years ago, we know that behind these honors lies the collective wisdom. The success of the proposal was based on in-depth research carried out through the CPPCC platform by organization at all levels of the CDL, with the support of the Central Committee of the CPC.

Beginning

As the cradle of Chinese civilization, an essential northern and northwestern China water source, and a significant ecological barrier and economic belt, the Yellow River has always been a government concern. Various issues related to the Yellow River have always been critical areas for the Central Committee of the CDL to advise and consult on.

From the mid-1980s to the late 1990s, Fei Xiaotong, former vice chairman of the Standing Committee of the National People's Congress and chairman of the Central Committee of the CDL, visited Henan on average once a year. In July 1998, Fei Xiaotong, who had just resigned as chairman of the Central Committee of the CDL, traveled thousands of miles to Henan which he had already visited more than ten times. At the symposium attended by the local United Front, the CPPCC, the CDL and the Yellow River Water Conservancy Committee, Fei affectionately told everyone that on the one hand, the Yellow River was drained and water resources saw severe shortage; on the other hand, people's lives and safety were seriously affected by floods of the Yellow River. To deal with this problem we had to rely on the concerted efforts of local party organization, administration, experts, and scholars, to find solutions to alleviate flooding. Fei Xiaotong also said that the Central Committee of the CDL was considering the comprehensive management measures for the middle and upper reaches of the Yellow River, and was ready to put forward specific suggestions to the Central Committee of the CPC to attract more attention to the issue from the top policymakers. In August of the same year, Xie Songkai, the former vice chairman of the Central Committee of the CDL, also came to Henan for an inspection, paying special attention to the ability of the Yellow River to resist extreme flooding and expressing his hopes that more research related to the management of the river could be done. The Henan Provincial Committee of the CDL and the members of the CDL who were working on the front line of the Yellow River were always concerned with the management and development of the Yellow River. They had conducted many investigations and organized seminars to provide suggestions for defending the mother river.

At the end of 1998, when the Central Committee of the CDL listened to the work report of the provincial organization during the working meeting, they found that the research report on the management of the Yellow River submitted by the Henan Provincial Committee of the CDL was closely related to the current situation, and it was feasible and particularly prominent. This proposal was highly thought of. The senior leaders of the Central Committee of the CDL, including Ding Shisun, Feng Zhijun, and Wu Xiuping, decided to submit the proposal for law-based Yellow River management to the CPPCC National Committee at the regular chairman's meeting.

At the meeting offering suggestions for the two sessions held in January 1999, the Central Committee of the CDL submitted the proposal to the Second Session of the 9th CPPCC National Committee. The proposal, which derived from 226 contributions submitted by affiliated organizations, and which had been polished and revised several times, was submitted by the Central Committee of the CDL to the CPPCC National Committee, and became one of the most prominent proposals of the year.

The Formation of the Proposal

After the proposal on the Yellow River was submitted, there was frequent communication between Beijing and Zhengzhou about it. The Central Committee of the CDL paid due attention to opinions and suggestions given by experts in the grassroots committee of the CDL who were front-line staff for Yellow River management.

To implement the instructions of the Central Committee of the CDL and collect basic information for major decision-making on the governance of the Yellow River, leaders of the Henan Provincial Committee of the CDL made a special trip to the Yellow River Commission to listen to the opinions of experts. The CDL members of the Henan Provincial Department of Water Resources and Zhengzhou Water Conservancy School also did a lot of work to provide information for the proposal. The CDL Yellow River Committee held several proposal meetings and actively participated in seminars on the management of the Yellow River organized by the CDL committee at the provincial level. The

The roaring Yellow River

CDL members of the Yellow River Committee also visited leaders and experts in the Hydrology Bureau, the Design Institute, and the Water Administration and Water Resources Bureau. They looked up a lot of relevant literature to sort out major issues on the governance of the Yellow River.

Members of the Henan Provincial Committee of the CDL and those working on the front line were deeply inspired and motivated. They organized experts and scholars to go to the Yellow River many times to investigate the suspended river section and bottomland to seek countermeasures. They discussed feasible solutions with experts and scholars day and night and gradually outlined the idea for harnessing and protecting the mother river. After more than a month of hard work, seven proposals were formulated, including "The Situation of Flood Control in the Lower Reaches of the Yellow River Is Serious, and It Is Still Necessary to Unremittingly Carry out the Construction of Flood Control Projects," "Formulate the Yellow River Law to Ensure the Management of the Yellow River in the New Century" and "Water Pollution in the Yellow River Is Serious and Powerful Governance Measures According to Law Is in Urgent Need," proposed by the Design Institute Branch of Yellow River Committee of the CDL; "The Rational Basis for the Development and Utilization of Water

Resources in the Yellow River Must Be Strengthened," written by the branch of the Hydrology Bureau of the CDL Yellow River Committee; "To Establish a Unified System for Managing the Yellow River Water Resources as Soon as Possible" and "Remediation of Wandering Watercourses in the Lower Yellow River after the Xiaolangdi Reservoir Is Put into Use," written by the branch of the Water Conservancy Science Research Institute of the Yellow River Committee of the CDL; "Henan Should Make Good Use of Water Resources from the Yellow River," drawn up by the branch of the unit directly under the CDL's Yellow River Committee.

After research, consideration and selection, the Central Committee of the CDL wrote the "Proposal on Increasing Investment to Manage the Yellow River by the Law" and submitted it to the Second Session of the 9th CPPCC National Committee. The proposal was quite concise, with three articles in just about three-hundred characters:

(1) Formulate the "Yellow River Law" as soon as possible, and all provinces and regions along the Yellow River should urgently manage and develop the Yellow River in an orderly manner. To achieve the organic combination of management concerned with the river basin, administrative area and industry, relevant issues along upstream and downstream areas, river banks, and regional and departmental interests should be coordinated in national legislation. Issues such as flood control and disaster reduction, soil and water conservation, siltation and poverty alleviation, resource development and environmental protection should be jointly dealt with.

(2) Take measures as soon as possible to solve the drying up of water flow in the Yellow River. Establish a unified water resources management agency, introduce methods to properly allocate water resources of the river and unify vertical datum; take the water-saving projects of the Yellow River Basin into consideration as a whole, integrate them into the national economic development plan, arrange investment at the national level, and make good use of matching funds at the provincial level and work on water conservation; adjust water prices as soon as possible; speed up the South-to-North Water Diversion Project.

(3) The state should increase investment in the management of the Yellow River. Before 1995, 100 million to 200 million yuan was invested in the construction of flood control projects annually. Up to 1999, only 300 million to 400 million yuan was added to the flood control project funds, which was far from fulfilling real needs. In the coming three years, it was estimated that at least 7 billion yuan would be needed. This would be a crucial support measure to fundamentally solve the flood damage problem in the Yellow River.

After the Proposal Was Adopted

After the two sessions, the Yellow River Commission obtained new funds allocated by the central government to supplement the funds for the management of the Yellow River. According to one staff member, when the Central Committee of the CDL went to Henan for a follow-up investigation, a leader of the Yellow River Commission was so happy and excited that he tightly gripped Feng Zhijun's hand and said, "Thank the CDL. Vice Chairman Feng, you may not know that after the proposal, the central government have allocated sufficient fund to support our work." Feng said cheerfully: "The Party and the government gave the money. We should thank the United Front Work Department and CPPCC for setting up the stage, and we cooperate and echo with them just at the right time and issue..."

Vice Chairman Feng's words humorously illustrated China's new type of political party relationship. The then chairman of the 9th CPPCC National Committee, was Li Ruihuan, once a worker. The vice chairman was Ye Xuanping, who presided over the executive work of the CPPCC. There was also Qian Weichang, a veteran scientist, who was elected vice-chairman of the CPPCC for the third time. Among the leaders of Henan Province, the deputy secretary of the Provincial Party Committee was Li Keqiang, one of the youngest provincial governors in China at that time. During the late 1990s, China's fiscal revenue was small, and almost all areas, such as science and technology, culture, education, health care and sports, were in urgent need of money. However, Zhu Rongji, who had just served as the Premier for a year, decided to allocate a sum of money to the Yellow River Committee of the Ministry of Water Resources to directly implement and realize the "Yellow River No. 1 Proposal." This shows the characteristics and advantages of multi-party cooperation.

To implement the proposal, after the two sessions, the Central Committee of the CDL assigned personnel to Henan to visit the Yellow River Water Conservancy Committee of the Ministry of Water Resources, and discussed with the leaders of the "Yellow River Committee" and the CDL experts to collect the opinions and suggestions of experts in Yellow River management, and jointly discuss the development strategy of the Yellow River Basin. The two sides exchanged views on the research on the development strategy of the Yellow River Basin and agreed on a plan for further cooperation.

In June 1999, at the invitation of the Henan Provincial Government and the Yellow River Committee, Feng Zhijun, the former vice chairman of the Central Committee of the CDL, went to Zhengzhou to negotiate with the Yellow River Committee and the Provincial Committee of the Henan League about the further implementation of the proposal. Zhao Wei, then deputy director of the United Front Work Department of the Henan Provincial Committee of the CPC, E Jingping, director of the Yellow River Commission, Feng Hongshun, chairman of the Henan Provincial Committee of the CDL and other leaders, as well as Yu Jian, Li Wenjia, Wang Xuehai, Wang Ling and other League members and experts attended the meeting to promote further implementation of "Proposal No. 1." Vice-Chairman Feng, on behalf of the Central Committee of the CDL, summed up the experience of how to achieve good results when participating in and deliberating politics. He concluded, "We must rely closely on grassroots organizations and the majority of League members, give full rein to the role of the group, and bring together the wisdom of the entire League."

The chairman office meeting of the CDL Central Committee also decided to invite Professor Feng Hongshun, then Chairman of the Henan Provincial Party Committee, to deliver a speech on the Yellow River issue on behalf of the Central Committee of the CDL at the Standing Committee of the CPPCC National Committee held in June 1999. The speech covered the importance of environmental protection and sustainable development, the countermeasures for preventing major floods of the Yellow River, and formulating relevant laws and regulations.

Looking Forward

On September 18, 2019, General Secretary Xi Jinping's "Speech at the Symposium on Ecological Protection and High-quality Development in the Yellow River Basin" pointed out that "protecting the Yellow River is a long-term plan for the great rejuvenation of the Chinese nation." "Promoting the ecological protection of the Yellow River Basin combined with high-quality development will not be achieved overnight. We must maintain patience and strategic determination, and hold onto the idea that we will not claim the credit but will always make sure to contribute our share to the success of the cause. We must plan for the future and work hard at present. A blueprint is drawn up and then realized by people from generation to generation to ensure that the Yellow River can benefit the people." The Yellow River is once again in the spotlight.

The Central Committee of the CDL actively responded to the call of the Central Committee of the CPC. "Ecological protection and high-quality development of the Yellow River Basin" was regarded as a critical topic in 2020. But besides the current issue, the CDL also pays attention to long-term development: suggestions on various issues about the Yellow River have been submitted to the Central Committee of the CPC and the State Council. We are well aware that under the leadership of the CPC, we will give full rein to the advantages of our political system and the characteristics of multi-party cooperation. We will also take it as a remarkable moment of historical and practical significance when we are committed to the governance and protection of our mother river and firmly set foot on a new journey.

(Contributed by the Central Committee of the CDL)

The Proposal to Add to the Constitution a Provision for "Multi-party Cooperation and Political Consultation System under the Leadership of the CPC"

17

PROFILE OF THE PRINCIPAL PROPOSER

WANG HONGCHANG (1921–2007), a native of Changshu, Jiangsu Province, joined the China National Democratic Construction Association (CNDCA) in January 1954 and served as a member and standing committee member of the Central Committee of the CNDCA, a member, standing committee member, deputy chairman, executive deputy chairman and honorary deputy chairman of the Shanghai Committee of the CNDCA, and the deputy secretary general of the Shanghai Municipal Committee of the CPPCC. From 1992 to 1997, he submitted 158 proposals to the CPPCC, many of which were adopted and implemented by the State Council or the relevant departments of the Shanghai Municipal Government. Wang was known as the "King of Proposals."

The Multi-party Cooperation and Political Consultation System under the Leadership of the CPC Is Written into the Constitution

The system of multi-party cooperation and political consultation under the leadership of the CPC is a fundamental political system in China. It was conceived during the Democratic Revolution Period, formed at the early stage of the founding of New China, and developed further since the reform and opening up. It is the inevitable choice in China's modern history, the inevitable result of the development of the New Democratic Revolution, and the objective requirement of the socialist revolution, construction and reform. In 1993, "The CPC-led system of multiparty cooperation and political consultation will exist and develop in the long run" was written into the Constitution and elevated as part of the national will in the Amendment to the Constitution of the People's Republic of China adopted at the First Session of the 8th National People's Congress (NPC). This move showcased to the world that the CPC and the other political parties firmly adhere to the multi-party cooperation and political consultation system under the leadership of the CPC, which is of great practical and far-reaching historical significance. The CNDCA has played an active role in promoting the inclusion of multi-party cooperation and political consultation system under the leadership of the CPC in the Constitution.

In 1993, as the initial proposer, Wang Hongchang, a member of the CNDCA, with Chen Mingshan, then a member of the Standing Committee of the CPPCC

National Committee and Vice Chairman of the CNDCA, submitted Proposal No. 0123 to the First Session of the 8th CPPCC National Committee, entitled "Proposal to Add to the Constitution a Provision on "Multi-party Cooperation and Political Consultation System under the Leadership of the CPC." The proposal suggested that there had been a great development in political and economic circumstances since the promulgation and implementation of the current Constitution. To meet the needs of the current situation, the National People's Congress had discussed and finalized some amendments to the Constitution, including the issues involved in the reform of the economic system and the political system. According to the spirit of Document No. 14 of the CPC Central Committee in 1989, in order to help uphold and improve the basic political system of multi-party cooperation and political consultation under the leadership of the CPC and give full play to its positive aspects, it was proposed that, in the partial revision of the Constitution, the following should be added. (1) the multi-party cooperation and political consultation system under the leadership of the Communist Party of China is a basic political system in China; (2) the guidelines of relationship between the Party and the other political parties are "Long term coexistence, mutual supervision, treating each other with sincerity, sharing weal and woe"; (3) the Party and the other political parties cooperate with each other, and share the common commitment to the cause of socialism; (4) make principle provisions of the legal status and terms of reference of the CPPCC in China's political system. The Legal Working Committee of the Standing Committee of the NPC handled the proposal and replied as follows on May 25: The multi-party cooperation and political consultation system under the leadership of the CPC has been written into the Constitution. Article 4 of the Amendment to the Constitution of the People's Republic of China adopted at the First Session of the 8th NPC stipulates that the following is added at the end of the tenth paragraph of the preamble of the Constitution: "The multi-party cooperation and political consultation system under the leadership of the CPC will exist and develop over a long period."

Proposal No. 0123 is not a random thought but the result of the CNDCA's long-term research on improving the multi-party cooperation system under the leadership of the CPC.

During the First Session of the 7th CPPCC National Committee, leaders of eight other political parties jointly held a press conference with Chinese and foreign journalists to answer questions on the status and role of multi-party cooperation and other political parties under the leadership of the CPC.

Long before the 13th CPC National Congress was held, and in line with the gestation process of China's economic and political system reform, a series of studies and discussions on improving the multi-party cooperation system under the leadership of the CPC were conducted within the political parties and the relevant departments of the Central Committee of the CPC. During the study process, the Central Committee of the CPC set up a special group to take charge of the leading work of drafting the documents. Sun Qimeng, then vice chairman of the Standing Committee of the NPC and chairman of the CDNCA Central Committee, participated in the work of the leading group and put forward many opinions and suggestions on behalf of the CNDCA Central Committee. At the Second Session of the 7th CPPCC National Committee in 1989, a CNDCA member made a speech in the name of CNDCA entitled "Progressively Improving, Enriching and Developing the Multi-party Cooperation System under the Leadership of the CPC on the Precondition of Adherence," addressing some misconceptions about the multi-party cooperation system in China in social practice and emphasizing the historical inevitability of adhering to the leadership of the CPC and multi-party cooperation, as well as the inextricable link between the two.

In December 1989, the "Opinions of the CPC Central Committee on Adhering to and Perfecting the Multi-party Cooperation and Political Consultation System under the Leadership of the Communist Party of China" ([1989] No. 14 Document by General Office of the CPC Central Committee) (hereafter Opinions) were officially promulgated and implemented. After it was issued, the CNDCA promptly notified the plenary session, requesting all its affiliated organizations to study the Opinions earnestly, and implement, practice and disseminate it in strenuous effort. At the subsequent National Committee of the CPPCC, the CNDCA made a speech entitled "Implementing the Opinions of the Central Committee of the CPC and Continuing to Strengthen the CPC Construction."

In February 1990, the "Opinions of the CPC Central Committee on Adhering to and Perfecting the Multi-party Cooperation and Political Consultation System under the Leadership of the CPC" was published and implemented.

In the proposed amendment to the Constitution in 1993, the issue of multi-party cooperation was not covered initially. The CNDCA proposed to add "multi-party cooperation and political consultation system under the leadership of the Communist Party of China" to the preamble of the Constitution. Before the First Session of the 8th CPPCC National Committee, the CNDCA conducted in-depth research on the issue of multi-party cooperation and the political consultation system under the leadership of the CPC should be written into the Constitution, and actively proposed suggestions. In January, 1993, Sun Qimeng invited a group of legal practitioners in the CNDCA or beyond to discuss the inclusion of the multi-party cooperation and political consultation system under the leadership of the CPC in the Constitution. Then, the Central Committee of the CNDCA carried out a related investigation and research. On February 14, the Central Committee of the CPC submitted to the Standing Committee of the 7th NPC a proposal on amending the national constitution, which did not cover the issue of multi-party cooperation. On February 22, the CNDCA entrusted Li Chonghuai to speak at the 30th meeting of the Standing Committee of the 7th NPC, suggesting that "the multi-party cooperation and political consultation system under the leadership of the CPC" be added to the preamble of the Constitution. On hearing his proposal, Chairman Wan Li said: "Li Chonghuai's proposal is excellent: This content should be added to the Constitution, and his speech should be presented to Qiao Shi (head of the Constitution amendment group)."

On March 1, 1993, the Central Committee of the CNDCA submitted to the Central Committee of the CPC a "Proposal on the Explicit Provision of the Multi-party Cooperation and Political Consultation System under the Leadership of the CPC in the Constitution," together with a letter from Sun Qimeng to Wen Jiabao, then an alternate member of the Political Bureau of the Central Committee of the CPC, Secretary of the Secretariat of the Central Committee of the CPC, and Director of the General Office of the Central Committee of the CPC. The letter mentioned: "According to the proposal of the Central Committee of the CPC, the Standing Committee of the 7th NPC has decided to put the amendment to the Constitution on the agenda of the upcoming First Session of the 8th NPC. The Central Committee of the CNDCA believes that the matter is crucial. As a participating party, it is responsible for contributing to the accomplishment of this important task." It was proposed that, after the release of the proposal of the Central Committee of the CPC to amend some parts of the Constitution of the People's Republic of China, the Central Committee of the CNDCA expressed its full support; at the same time, it was necessary that "the multi-party cooperation and political consultation system under the leadership of the CPC be clearly written into the Constitution," and there were four reasons for this: First, the multi-party cooperation and political consultation system under the leadership of the CPC was an indispensable and important part of Deng Xiaoping's theory on building socialism with Chinese characteristics. Second, including the multi-party cooperation and political consultation system under the leadership of the CPC in the Constitution was more conducive to its implementation and to strengthening the ruling status and role of the CPC. Third, the political party system was the cornerstone of the political systems of modern countries. Fourth, adding the multi-party cooperation and political consultation system under the leadership of the CPC in the Constitution was just at the right moment that couldn't be missed. After the proposal was put forward, at the democratic consultation meeting chaired by Jiang Zemin on March 6, 1993, Sun Qimeng again proposed that the multi-party cooperation and political consultation system led by the CPC be written into the Constitution. The proposal was accepted by the Central Committee of the CPC. On March 14, the Central Committee of the CPC submitted to the Presidium of the First Session of the 8th NPC a "Supplementary Proposal on Amending the Constitution." Its first article suggested adding the sentence, "The multi-party cooperation and political consultation system under the leadership of the CPC will exist and develop over a long period," into the tenth paragraph in the preamble of the Constitution. On March 18, the Presidium of the 8th NPC held its second meeting and decided to submit the "Supplementary Proposal on Amending the Constitution" to the 8th NPC for voting. All delegates of the First Session of the 8th NPC voted to adopt the proposal.

The long-term existence and development of the multi-party cooperation and political consultation system under the leadership of the CPC were written into the Constitution, and this laid a solid foundation for the legalization and standardization of multi-party cooperation. Since then, the cause of multi-party partnership in China has become more stable and has gone further along the road of legalization, institutionalization, standardization and routinization. In 1997, the 15th National Congress of the CPC raised the importance of the adherence to and improvement of the multi-party cooperation and political consultation system under the leadership of the CPC to the level of keeping to the path of socialist political advancement with Chinese characteristics. It included it in the basic program of the primary stage of socialism, proposing to continue to promote the institutionalization and standardization of political consultation, democratic supervision and participation in political affairs. Since the 16th National Congress of the CPC, the Central Committee of the CPC has kept striving for the future based on the heritage and the pace with the time, focusing on the construction of socialist political civilization, and formulated "Opinions of the Central Committee of the CPC on Further Strengthening the Construction of the Multi-party Cooperation and Political Consultation System under the Leadership of the CPC," "Opinions of the Central Committee of the CPC on Strengthening the Work of the CPPCC," "Opinions of the Central Committee of the CPC on Consolidating and Strengthening the United Front in the New Century and the New Stage," "Opinions of the Central Committee of the CPC on Strengthening the Construction of Socialist Consultative Democracy," "Regulations on the Work of the United Front of the CPC (for Trial Implementation)," "Implementation Opinions on Strengthening Party Consultations," "Opinions on Strengthening the Work of the Party Construction of the People's Political Consultative Conference in the New Era" and "Opinions of the Central Committee of the CPC on Strengthening the Construction of Socialist Participating Parties with Chinese Characteristics." The cause of multi-party cooperation in China has entered a new stage of development.

(Contributed by the Central Committee of the CNDCA)

The Proposal on Foreign Aid in the Health Sector and Active Participation in Global Health Endeavors

18

PROFILE OF THE PRINCIPAL PROPOSER

WANG YU, Doctor of Medicine and Doctor of Science, is a professor at Tsinghua University and former director of the Chinese Center for Disease Control and Prevention (China CDC). He was a deputy to the 17th National Congress of CPC and a member of the 11th and 12th CPPCC National Committee. He served as director of Beijing Medical University Hepatology Institute, vice president of Beijing Medical University, and deputy director of Peking University Health Science Center (PKUHSC). He once administrated in administrating biological medicine technology at the Ministry of Science and Technology of the PRC. He was a rewarded the National Science Fund for Distinguished Young Scholars and is entitled to the special government allowances by the State Council. He won a special prize and a first prize in China's State Science and Technology Progress Award.

Health Cooperation within the Context of Globalization

On December 1st, 2016, President Ernest Bai Koroma, who had traveled from the Republic of Sierra Leone in West Africa to China, took time out of his tight schedule to visit the headquarters of the China CDC in Changping District, Beijing. He met with Chinese public health professionals who had been to Sierra Leone to participate in the fight against the Ebola epidemic. He warmly shook

On December 1, 2016, President Koroma of the Republic of Sierra Leone visited the Chinese Center for Disease Control and Prevention and presented the Center with a painting reflecting scenes from the country's celebration of its victory over the Ebola epidemic.

hands with team members, expressing his gratitude with repeated "Thank you!" He also presented a precious watercolor painting by a Sierra Leonean artist to the China CDC. This artwork depicted local youth singing and dancing to celebrate the country's victory over the Ebola epidemic. It vividly recorded the historical moment when the World Health Organization (WHO) announced the end of Sierra Leone's Ebola on March 17, 2016.

President Koroma's visit to China CDC highlights China's achievements in foreign health assistance and global health cooperation, and its joint efforts with other countries to tackle the global public health crisis.

In recent years, against the backdrop of economic globalization, China has begun to play a growing role in promoting global health. The Chinese medical teams went to Nigeria, Pakistan and other Asian and African countries to participate in the worldwide fight against polio in 2011–2012. They also offered unprecedented assistance in the fight against the Ebola epidemic in Africa. Reviewing these facts, I submitted a proposal titled "Foreign Aid in the Health Sector and Active Participation in Global Health Endeavors" during the First Session of the 12th CPPCC National Committee in 2013. The proposal not only reflected the pace of reform and opening up in China's health sector but also pointed out necessary conditions and requirements for China's participation in global public health cooperation, and was expected to promote cooperation in this regard.

China's Presence in Global Health Cooperation

In 1980, the WHO announced that smallpox was eliminated from the world due to vaccination. It was a plague that had ravaged humankind for thousands of years and caused countless deaths, disability, and disfigurement. That means children worldwide would no longer need a bovine vaccine to prevent smallpox, and no one would have lifelong regrets due to the facial pox left by the disease.

That was human's first victory in eradicating a severe infectious disease; the success greatly encouraged global health workers. In 1988, the WHO, international non-profit organizations and charitable foundations decided the next goal would be eliminating poliomyelitis, commonly known as polio, a disease resulting from infection by the poliovirus infection and also causing human, children in particular, death and disability.

Like smallpox, the poliovirus only infects humans. As long as people are vaccinated, the disease can be prevented until it is ultimately eliminated. The WHO has collaborated with the United Nations Children's Fund (UNICEF), an international non-governmental organization Rotary International, the US Centers for Disease Control and Prevention (US CDC), and the Gates Foundation, which later joined and became the key donor, to form the Global Polio Eradication Initiative (GPEI). The Initiative aims to raise funds and organize on-site assistance to carry out a polio eradication campaign worldwide. With the widespread vaccination, the number of new infection cases worldwide has dropped sharply. By 2018, 30 years after the campaign, Africa had successfully eradicated wild poliovirus (WPV). Only Pakistan and Afghanistan, reported 33 new cases that year. Human beings were close to the success of eradicating poliovirus.

As early as 1994, China had wiped out wild poliovirus from the country. As the largest developing country in the world, China's accomplishments in the fight against poliovirus during a time when the country's capita income was still meager, were a significant contribution to the global polio eradication efforts. With the success of the reform and opening up, China's policymakers have realized that the country's public health strategy should benefit not only domestic people but also others worldwide. This is not only to help other developing countries but also a prerequisite for the goal of ending the country's annual vaccinations of 16 million newborns as promptly as possible. Our ultimate goal is that China can join the global major force in the field of public health as soon as possible and take a new role as a health aid supplier. In particular, China should not be absent from the final global efforts to eradicate polio. When it comes to the moment of victory in the fight against polio, Chinese medical personnel are expected to be among those great fighters.

Active participation in worldwide polio eradication efforts is supposed to be the best attempt to join the global health cause. In 2011, the China CDC began such an attempt. Within the framework of the WHO, China CDC worked closely with the American counterpart and dispatched medical personnel to join the working groups in the three African countries, including Nigeria, Namibia, and Ethiopia, to guide local efforts on vaccination and to get more information about local vaccination work. Given various constraints at the time, only one immunization expert was sent to each country from China. After the successful attempt, China sent ten experts from the national and provincial CDCs to Pakistan to participate in a three-month intensive polio vaccination campaign organized by the WHO. The China CDC professionals were faced with arduous tasks. They had to visit villages and alleys to inspect and guide vaccination in the scorching heat above 40°C. Moreover, they had to work under the protection of armed local police in case of terrorist assaults.

The Chinese public health team didn't have much experience in going abroad and working with their international professional counterparts. Besides the limited experience and talent pool, the most prominent problem for the Chinese team was the lack of smooth communications. In response to these issues, my proposal of "Foreign Aid in the Health Sector and Active Participation in Global Health Endeavors" included the following suggestions: making participation in global public health cooperation an important part of China's international health strategy; developing preferential policies and incentives to encourage professionals' active participation; organizing training to improve the foreign language proficiency and other skills for the people dispatched on public health missions abroad.

China's Prominent Role in the Fight against Ebola in Africa

China began to dispatch medical professionals to other countries many years ago. Since the 1960s, more than 16,000 persons have been dispatched to 47 African countries. They provided countless locals with almost free medical services, winning accolades from the recipient countries and the international community. These medical aid services have promoted people-to-people exchanges and friendship between China and these countries. The previously dispatched medical teams were to assist in the treatment of patients. Amidst economic and social development, African countries have paid more attention to disease prevention and control and public health concerns such as AIDS, tuberculosis, malaria, and the eradication of polio, as well as outbreaks of infectious diseases, and they are in urgent need of public health support in those regards.

In the spring of 2014, the most violent Ebola epidemic in history broke out in three West African countries – Guinea, Sierra Leone, and Liberia. Although there had been more than 30 outbreaks since the discovery of the Ebola virus in 1976, they all occurred in remote and enclosed areas in central Africa, where infected persons could not leave their residence. The victims were either killed by the disease or survived by chance, and the impact on the outside world was limited. However, in June and July 2014, the outbreak, originally in the remote mountainous areas of southeastern Guinea gradually spread to the densely populated capitals of the three West African countries, resulting in a large number of infectious cases in a short period. On August 8th, the WHO declared the Ebola epidemic in West Africa a Public Health Emergency of International Concern (PHEIC), and the impact this time went global.

The largest-scale outbreak of Ebola plagued the poorest countries on the list of 189 economies of the United Nations Development Program. It was the first time the virus spread in metropolitan areas, with a fatality rate close to 50% and the death toll exceeding the total number of previous epidemics. Besides, the cases even spread to developed countries outside Africa; these concerns called for global support and assistance.

At a meeting held by the national health department, I suggested sending medical assistance teams to West African countries to help control the epidemic and participate in the global attempt to tackle the public health crisis. People held different opinions on my suggestion. The main concern of those who disagreed was that our public health workers did not have the experience and ability to treat the disease, and were unclear about what they could do there.

Because of my experience in international cooperation on polio eradication, I proposed that I could lead an advance team to visit the West African countries hit by the epidemic as soon as possible. Fighting the epidemic was a pressing task like firefighting, allowing no delay. Following the decision of the leadership to assist Sierra Leone first, on September 1, I led the advance team of 9 members to depart from Beijing for Freetown, the capital of the Republic of Sierra Leone. Due to the outbreak, almost all major airlines suspended flights from and to the three countries in West Africa. We had to detour to France, take the Air France flight to Casablanca, Morocco, then change to the flight of Royal Air Maroc to Monrovia, the capital of Liberia, the only flight that would stop at Freetown.

Due to many canceled flights, Casablanca Airport was disappointingly empty and quiet. I could not help but think of the well-known Rick's Cafe, a romantic place with splendid stories in the classic movie *Casablanca*, feeling that travelers should have filled the terminal building just for the movie's sake.

Thanks to China's Ambassador to Sierra Leone and the Commercial Counselor, we visited government officials such as the Minister of Health and the Minister of Foreign Affairs of Sierra Leone. We learned in detail about the epidemic and their urgent needs. We then introduced the Chinese government's assistance program to help Sierra Leone fight the epidemic. We spent lots of efforts looking for proper sites to set up a mobile P3 laboratory that would be transported from China by air. Our goal was to provide the most needed virus detection methods and safe laboratories to mitigate the outbreak as soon as

To set up a mobile biosafety P3 laboratory and a permanent biosafety laboratory, the advance team and officials from the Ministry of Health of Sierra Leone, and Zou Xiaoming, China's Commercial Counselor in Sierra Leone, inspected a site in a newly cleared jungle.

possible. Accompanied by government officials such as the deputy minister of Health of Sierra Leone, we inspected many sites including wild jungles for a fixed biosafety level 3 (P3) laboratory. Finally, we selected the neighboring area of the Sierra Leone-China Friendship Hospital sponsored by China. This location was also ideal for long-term cooperation in multiple fields of public health.

President Koroma received all the advance team members at the Presidential Palace and warmly expressed gratitude to the Chinese government. He said that China took the lead in sending a team of public health experts to provide support and assistance at the most critical moment of the epidemic when Sierra Leone needed help the most. Either morally or materially, China showed itself as a responsible major country and set up a good example for others.

As the Chinese public health teams came to Sierra Leone one after another, we achieved outstanding results, from working in the mobile P3 laboratory for Ebola virus testing, carrying out health education and training in the epidemic-stricken communities, building the first biosafety level 3 laboratory in West Africa, to collaborating with the professionals from the United States and other countries to study the virus infection. Due to the impact of the epidemic and the tight time limit, the materials needed to build the laboratory could not be obtained locally. They were all prefabricated in China and delivered by a large transport airplane. In only 87 days, the laboratory was completed, certified by experts from the WHO, and put into use. When visiting the bright and comfortable laboratory built in accordance with international biosafety standards, President Koroma and international experts in Sierra Leone gave high remarks. The China CDC sent 149 experts in 17 groups, tested more than 4,000 Ebola specimens, and provided public health training to more than 6,000 locals, including healthcare workers, community residents, teachers, and armed police officers. Model communities were established in three villages hit hard by the epidemic. All these progresses marked a great success for China's public health professionals in their first endeavor to join global public health cooperation.

Global Health Needs Multilateral Cooperation Mechanism

In 2015, China's National Health and Family Planning Commission and the United States Department of Health and Human Services (HHS) renewed the memorandum of health cooperation signed in 1978. It was modified with an added clause: encourage China and US CDC professionals to cooperate in a third country. This highlighted the active and open attitude of the Chinese government towards global health cooperation. In September of the same year, the Outcome List of President Xi Jinping's State Visit to the United States (94 Items) pledged joint efforts to improve public health capacity globally. It stated that "the two sides intend to jointly work with the African Union and African Union Member States in establishing the Africa Center for Disease Control and Prevention, and collaborate with governments of countries in West Africa to strengthen national capacities to deal with public health."

Under China's macro policy of further opening up and cooperation, Chinese experts collaborated with their American counterparts to fight the Ebola epidemic and conducted scientific research in Sierra Leone. After that, they went to the African Union headquarters in Ethiopia to assist with the construction of the African Center for Disease Control and Prevention. The fruitful multilateral cooperation has been acclaimed many times by the heads of governments from China and the U.S., becoming a new highlight in health cooperation between the two.

The proposals by the CPPCC National Committee members have played an essential role in promoting the active participation of Chinese public health professionals in global health cooperation. The National Committee leaders and members care much about the work of health aid to Africa and have adopted various methods to carry out research and promote the work. In 2017, the CPPCC National Committee held biweekly meetings on improving and strengthening China's health assistance to Africa. To ensure the success of the conference, the Central Committee of the Chinese Peasants and Workers Democratic Party and the Committee on Foreign Affairs of the CPPCC National Committee organized dedicated teams to conduct research in Beijing, Shanghai, Hubei, and Shanxi. I participated in the study in Beijing and Shanghai, and had extensive discussions and consultations, based on my practice and experience in recent years, with foreign affairs departments at different levels, hospital leaders, and medical workers who had participated in public health missions in Africa. At the biweekly meeting, the committee members put forward their opinions and suggestions on issues related to health assistance for African countries, such as the institutional mechanism, planning, assistance model, improved benefits for medical team members, and organized training for personnel sent abroad. After the meeting, the National Health Commission of PRC and other relevant departments issued documents concerning new institutional measures to improve and strengthen the work of medical teams for foreign aid.

(Contributed by Wang Yu, member of the 11th and 12th CPPCC National Committee)

Index

high-income earners, 31, 33
high-quality development, 73, 184
Hong Kong, 75, 77–85, 88–89, 91, 94–97
Hou Renzhi, 125, 127–34, 149–50
Hubei, 9, 13, 15, 204
Hu Heyan, 18, 21
Hu Jintao, 9, 11, 89
human civilization, 127, 137, 144, 159
Hunan, 9, 119
Hu Shuguang, 22
Hu Zhaozhou, 13, 18, 20–21, 23

I

individual income tax, 27–33
infrastructure, 56, 61, 63, 93, 140
inhalable particulate matter, 167
innovation-driven development, 83
International Academy of Brand Science, 72–73
International Organization for Standardization (ISO), 69, 71, 73
international standards for brand evaluation, 68, 71
Internet Protocol version 6 (IPv6), 83

J

Jiangsu, 3, 10, 49, 157, 185
Jiang Zemin, 192
Jin Bintong, 17–18, 21
Jiusan Society, 49, 52, 60
joint proposal, 17–19, 69, 127, 129, 131, 133, 155
juvenile delinquency, 120–21

K

Kang Keqing, 115, 117–18

L

land resources transfer, 8

Law on the Prevention of Juvenile Delinquency, 120, 123
Law on the Protection of Minors, 120–23
Liang Sicheng, 133
Li Bin, 49, 52–54
Li Chonghuai, 15, 191
Li Keqiang, 71, 173, 182
Li Peng, 47
Li Ruihuan, 20, 182
Liu Feng, 147, 151–53, 155, 160–61
Liu Pingjun, 69–70, 73
Li Zhiyong, 12
Luo Zhewen, 131–34, 149–51, 156

M

Macao Special Administrative Region (MSAR), 85, 88–89, 92–93, 95
market economy, 19, 29
medical and health system reform, 110
middle-income class, 30
Ministry of Education, 56, 105
Ministry of Finance (MOF), 9–10, 31–32, 56, 91, 146
Ministry of Health, 110, 169, 202
Ministry of Water Conservancy and Electric Power, 43–44, 47
Ministry of Water Resources, 182–83
moderately prosperous society, 55, 63
Mount Tai, 134
multilateral cooperation, 204
multi-level responsibility system, 171
multi-party cooperation and political consultation system, 95, 187–88, 191–93

N

Namibia, 199
National Air Quality and Public Health Protection Project, 171

209

LAI MING, a standing committee member and deputy secretary general of the 13th National Committee of the Chinese People's Political Consultative Conference (CPPCC), also serves as deputy director of the Committee on Proposals of CPPCC and vice chairman of the 12th to 14th Central Committee of the Jiusan Society. Being a professor and doctoral supervisor, he is a member of the Advisory Committee of the National High Technology Research and Development Program (briefly HTRDP Program or 863 Program). He was the vice president of the Chongqing University of Architecture (now Chongqing University) and director of the Science and Technology Department of the former Ministry of Construction.